Arts, Entertainment, & Christian Values

PROBING THE HEADLINES THAT IMPACT YOUR FAMILY

Jerry Solomon
General Editor

kregel
PUBLICATIONS

Grand Rapids, MI 49501

Arts, Entertainment, & Christian Values: Probing the Headlines That Impact Your Family

© 2000 by Probe Ministries

Published by Kregel Publications, a division of Kregel, Inc., P.O. Box 2607, Grand Rapids, MI 49501. Kregel Publications provides trusted, biblical publications for Christian growth and service. Your comments and suggestions are valued.

For more information about Kregel Publications, visit our web site: www.kregel.com

Library of Congress Cataloging-in-Publication Data
Solomon, Jerry.
   Arts, entertainment, & Christian values: probing the headlines that impact your famliy / edited by Jerry Solomon.
     p.   cm.—
Includes bibliographical references.
   1. Mass media—Religious aspects—Christianity.
2. Christianity and culture.   I. Title.
P94.A47   1999   261.5'2—dc 21   99-43118
                                                CIP

ISBN 0-8254-2032-6

Printed in the United States of America

1 2 3 4 5 / 04 03 02 01 00

Contents

Foreword

Our culture is awash in worldviews, each competing for our attention and allegiance. How should we, as Christians, relate to our culture? How do we make sense of competing worldviews? These are significant questions deserving thoughtful answers. The Issues in Focus series in general, and this book in particular, seek to provide some answers that we can immediately apply to our daily lives.

Culture surrounds us and, in many ways, makes life worth living. Yet, often we fail to understand the impact it is having on us. A Chinese proverb asks, "Why is a fish the last one to ask about water?" Fish cannot tell you about water because they live in it. What water is to fish, culture is to us. There is a war of worldviews taking place. Various sets of assumptions and presuppositions affect us in conscious and unconscious ways. They direct our thoughts. They govern our behavior. We need to step back and consider the influence our culture exerts on us. We also need clear guidelines on how we, in turn, can have an impact on our culture.

The following chapters provide a "road map" through these conflicting worldviews. They remind us that as Christian disciples we should not conform to the world but are to transform our minds through the renewing power of Christ (Romans 12:2).

I commend this book and encourage you, as you read it, to consider how you will be the salt of the earth and the light of the world (Matthew 5:13–16).

KERBY ANDERSON
PRESIDENT OF PROBE MINISTRIES

Contributors

Don Closson is the director of administration for Probe Ministries as well as a vital part of Probe's research team. He received a B.S. in education from Southern Illinois University, an M.S. in educational administration from Illinois State University, and an M.S. (cum laude) in biblical studies from Dallas Theological Seminary. He served as a public school teacher and administrator before joining Probe Ministries in 1986 as a research associate in the field of education.

Todd A. Kappelman is a field associate with Probe Ministries. He received a B.A. and an M.A.B.S. in religion and Greek from Dallas Baptist University and an M.A. in humanities/philosophy from the University of Dallas. Currently he is pursuing a Ph.D. in philosophy and religion at the University of Dallas. He has served as assistant director of the Trinity Institute, a study center devoted to Christian thought and inquiry. He has been the managing editor of *The Antithesis,* a bimonthly publication devoted to the critique of foreign and independent film. His central area of expertise is Continental philosophy, especially nineteenth/twentieth century and postmodern thought. Todd also is working on "alternative ministries" for Probe. He does all the coordinating and scheduling of speakers for the *Tuesday Night Forum at Club Dada.* This is a weekly philosophy, theology, and ethics forum in the "Deep Ellum" arts district of downtown Dallas. Todd is the senior speaker and participates regularly in the rotation.

Jerry Solomon is the field director and *Mind Games* coordinator at Probe Ministries. He received a B.A. (summa cum laude) in Bible and an M.A. (cum laude) in history and theology from Criswell College. He also has attended the University of North Texas, Canal Zone College, and Lebanon Valley College. In the past, Jerry has worked as a youth pastor. He is the author of *Sheep Among Wolves.*

Rick Wade is a research associate for Probe. He has a B.A. in communications (radio broadcasting) from Moody Bible Institute and an M.A. (cum laude) in Christian thought (theology/philosophy of religion) from Trinity Evangelical Divinity School, where his studies culminated in a thesis on the apologetics of Carl F. H. Henry.

Jimmy Williams is the founder and former president of Probe Ministries. He is currently minister-at-large. Jimmy has been involved in ministry to young adults and Christians of all ages for forty years. He graduated with a B.A. from Southern Methodist University and a Th.M. from Dallas Theological Seminary. He has pursued inter-disciplinary doctoral studies (A.B.D.) in humanities at the University of Texas at Dallas. He was involved in the Campus Crusade for Christ ministry from 1961 to 1973.

Part 1
Culture

1

Christians and Culture

Jerry Solomon

What do you think of when you hear the word *culture?* Perhaps you think of the arts. You might picture people's clothing, their eating habits, their language, their religion, their architecture, or a host of other perceptions. One of the most succinct definitions of the term *culture* is "that which man does beyond biological necessity."[1] Obviously, such a definition indicates the importance of the term. Our lives are lived within culture. There is no escaping this thing called culture. But how is a Christian to respond to it?

Church history demonstrates that one of the constant struggles of Christians, both individually and corporately, is with culture. Paul, for example, wrote two letters to Christians who lived in Corinth, a very challenging environment. Where should we stand in relation to our own culture? Inside? Outside? Should we ignore it? Become isolated from it? Should we attempt to transform it?

Paradigms of Culture

In 1949, a theologian named Richard Niebuhr delivered a series of lectures titled *Christ and Culture.*[2] Subsequently his thoughts were published, and the book has become a classic. Niebuhr's text focuses on five paradigms that show

how Christians have dealt with culture. A brief survey of these paradigms can help us see ourselves and perhaps challenge us to consider changing the way we look at the world around us.

First, the phrase *Christ against culture* describes those who choose to isolate themselves from the surrounding world. A descriptive contemporary phrase might be "the holy huddle" of Christians who dialogue among themselves but no one else. Second, the *Christ of culture* perspective is exactly the opposite of *Christ against culture* because it attempts to bring culture and Christianity together, regardless of their differences. Third, the *Christ above culture* position attempts to synthesize the issues of the culture with the answer of Christian revelation. Fourth, *Christ and culture in paradox* refers to those who understand the tension between the Christian's responsibility to both the cultural and the spiritual realms. Fifth, *Christ the transformer of culture* describes those who strive "to convert the values and goals of secular culture into the service of the kingdom of God."[3]

Which of these paradigms describes your relationship with the culture in which you live? Or perhaps you have another paradigm to offer. No doubt we could engage in debate about the merits and demerits of all such paradigms. But since we can't do that at the moment, let's agree that we should at least give attention to our place in culture.

As Christians we are to observe and analyze culture and make decisions regarding our proper actions and reactions within it. A struggle is in progress and the stakes are high. But if we want to struggle meaningfully and with some hope of having influence, we must be thoughtful and informed.

Our work through Probe Ministries is dedicated to the proposition that the Lord can use Christians as salt and light. God has called us to offer a voice to both the Christian and the non-Christian communities. We have attempted to do this for the glory of God. Our involvement in the non-Christian community presents a special challenge. We have devoted much prayer and study on the task of finding the right principles before we engage our world.

Biblical Precepts

Unless you live in a cave, you have had to deal with the culture around you. You have sensed the need to think about how you might glorify God as you react to your culture. Or you may have experienced times of mental and spiritual trauma as you realized the sinful nature of what you experience around you. If you choose to interact with your culture, you should consider certain principles.

The first such principle is the need for biblical precepts. Our minds should be filled with God's ideas before we interact with the culture. This is an understandable and universally stated declaration among evangelical Christians. Experience tells us that we need to give life to the declaration. Are we responding to our culture based on biblical precepts, or is our response based on other sources? Are we using a Christian worldview, or are we unwittingly using a naturalistic worldview, for example? When we discuss things as Christians, do we focus on Scripture, no matter what we might be discussing? "Contemporary Christianity is all too frequently shaped by the fact that when we meet we do so in an atmosphere resembling that of a committee or caucus, where the style is political and tactical, hardly scholarly, and almost never devotional or genuinely spiritual."[4] Do we give serious attention "to the sacred text as the firm and only basis on which life and decisions should be based?"[5] Indeed, without the "sacred text" evangelicals are left to grapple with their culture in much the same manner as those who do not claim allegiance to that text.

To affirm the primacy of Scripture in a cultural critique, the Christian should "read" his culture in the light of the Bible. Proper recognition of the surrounding world is necessary before we can address it properly. In other words, we need a biblical "lens" through which we can see the culture. The light of God's Word needs to be focused on the questions at hand. For example, most people tend to "secularize" life. Most of us live, work, and play in the secular sphere. But "secularism" refers to a way of life that "excludes all considerations drawn from a belief in God or in a future state."[6] Harry Blamires, a protégé of C. S. Lewis and an astute cultural critic, offers an insightful critique of secularism.

> The secularist's position can be defined only in negatives. There is no life except this life in time. There is no order of being except that which we explore with our senses and our instruments. There is no condition of well-being except that of healthy and comfortable life in time. There is no God to be worshipped, for no God created us. There is no God to propitiate, for there is no God to offend. There is no reward to be sought and no punishment to be avoided except those which derive from earthly authority. There is no law to be obeyed except those

>which earthly authority imposes or earthly
>prudence recommends.[7]

Obviously, Blamires's observations are the result of seeing secularism through a scriptural lens. Biblical precepts allow him to offer such a critique. His example can be an encouragement for us. May God guide us as we apply biblical precepts to evaluate our culture.

Cultural Bias

What do you think of the culture in which you live? In particular, what do you think of the broader American culture in which your subculture is found? For example, are you comfortable with the slogan, "America: love it or leave it"? Or do you tend to think of certain other cultures as pristine, even if you've never visited them?

The second principle is focused on what I call cultural bias. If we are to interact with cultures other than our own, and if we seek honestly to evaluate our own, we must be cautious of biases.

Carl F. H. Henry, a great theologian, apologist, and cultural critic, enumerated what he calls twenty fantasies of a secular society. One of these includes the thought that God "will protect the United States and its people from catastrophic disaster because of our commitment to freedom, generosity, and goodness." Dr. Henry writes, "For many, God is an ever-living George Washington who serves invisibly as the father of our country. This vague political theology assumes that America can never drift irrecoverably beyond divine approval, and that the nation is intrinsically exempt from severe and final divine judgment." Another fantasy is "that the American people are essentially good at heart in a world whose inhabitants are more prone to evil."[8]

Anthropologist Charles Kraft responds to such thinking by writing that "much of the Christian populace has simply continued to assume that such features of our society as monogamy, democracy, our type of educational system, individualism, capitalism, the 'freedoms,' literacy, technological development, military supremacy, and so on, are all products of our association with God and therefore can be pointed to as indications of the superiority of our culture over all other cultures."[9]

Missionaries who serve in cultures other than their own can speak to the danger of such fantasies. But we don't have to be foreign missionaries to experience the effects of cultural bias. The United States has become such a multicultural environment that Christians can and must understand the importance of being alert to it.

Interaction, Not Accommodation

A third principle of cultural evaluation focuses on the need for interaction but not accommodation. There should be no fear in this if we are using biblical precepts, the first of our principles. But we need to be alert to the ways in which we can become enmeshed in the culture. In addition, we should be accountable to one another by offering warnings when we observe such entanglement.

If evangelicals neglect cultural interaction, they leave numerous important facets of contemporary life without the light of truth they can offer. A cursory reading of post-Enlightenment history will demonstrate the progressive decrease of evangelical interaction and the subsequent lack of influence in strategic areas of culture. For example, American higher education has been guided by principles that leave Christian theism out of the picture.

It is crucial, though, that such interaction take place

with a sense of accountability. The person who enters the culture without respect for the ideological dangers that reside there will prove to be foolish. The ideas, the sense of progress, and the pride of cultural accomplishment can lead us to give credit to man instead of to God. May God receive praise as He uses us to touch our culture!

A Revolutionary Vision

The word *revolution* tends to have a negative connotation for most of us. A revolutionary most often is seen as someone who engenders rebellion and chaos. But a Christian's response to culture should include a positive revolutionary mind-set. Christian thought and life should state ideas that exhibit Christ's revolutionary vision for all people. A type of pluralism that tempts us to negate Christianity's claims and absolutes should not persuade Christians. Donald Bloesch speaks to this tension by juxtaposing what he calls prophetic religion and culture religion. He writes, "Our choice today is between a prophetic religion and a culture religion. The first is anchored in a holy God who infinitely transcends every cultural and religious form that testifies to him. The second absolutizes the cultural or mythical garb in which God supposedly meets us."[10] Our interaction with culture must have a prophetic voice. It must speak boldly to the culture with the knowledge that the source of its proclamations is the sovereign God.

This means that Christians should not relegate their lives to what may be called a "Christian ghetto" or "holy huddle." Too many Christians live "a split life: they are forced to use many words and images that have a private meaning for them with which they are unable or unwilling to enrich the fund of public experience."[11] They may have a revolutionary vision and prophetic zeal, but too often these are directed toward their "ghetto" instead of the surrounding culture. To quote an old cliché, "They are preaching to the choir."

Notice how often conversations among Christians concentrate on problems presented by the surrounding culture. For example, discussion may focus on the latest outrage in the entertainment industry; or the newest bit of intrigue in Washington; or concerns about the sex education emphases in public schools; or controversies surrounding issues of abortion, euthanasia, cloning, homosexuality, or child abuse; or a host of other topics. Then notice if the conversants offer constructive suggestions. Do they give attention to the ways in which the Christian community might respond to such issues based on biblical precepts? Too often, such a scenario does not include positive, revolutionary, cultural interaction.

J. Lesslie Newbigin, a perceptive cultural critic, offers two propositions regarding a Christian's revolutionary vision. First, Newbigin states that he would not see Christians just "in that corner of the private sector which our culture labels 'religion,' but rather in the public sector where God's will as declared in Jesus Christ is either done or not done in the daily business of nations and societies, in the councils of governments, the boardrooms of transnational corporations, the trade unions, the universities, and the schools." Second, "I would place [in the public sector] the recovery of that apocalyptic strand of the New Testament teaching without which Christian hope becomes merely hope for the survival of the individual and there is no hope for the world."[12] Christianity is not to be privatized; it applies to all people in all places at all times.

If we choose to take Newbigin's propositions seriously,

we must not be naïve about the response we will receive. At this moment in American history, the public sector is often antagonistic toward a Christian voice. Therefore, we should not be surprised when we are rejected. Instead, if we are stating God's ideas, we should rejoice, as did the early Christians when they suffered for Christ (Acts 5:41). When truth rubs shoulders with untruth, friction is often the result.

Glorifying God

The words *whatever* and *all* are enormous. Can you think of something more than *whatever* or *all*? When the apostle Paul wrote his first letter to the church in Corinth he used these terms to describe how they should glorify God: "Whether, then, you eat or drink or *whatever* you do, do *all* to the glory of God" (1 Cor. 10:31, emphasis added). Pagan Corinth certainly provided many opportunities for early Christians to learn how to respond to their culture. The same is true for Christians in our time. We live in and associate with a culture that presents challenges constantly. We are to glorify God in all we do, regardless of those challenges. "Where God is acknowledged as the Creator, man knows that the ultimate meaning of His creatures is the same as the meaning of all life: the glory of God and the service of men."[13] Our work within the culture and our influence on it are part of what God will judge. Therefore, these works are important.

We are to remind ourselves and tell the culture that "the prophetic church witnesses to the breaking into history of a higher righteousness; it points people to a higher law."[14] Carl F. H. Henry emphasizes this point in a passage concerning education, but the implications cover much more.

> The drift of twentieth century learning can
> be succinctly summarized in one statement:
> Instead of recognizing [God] as the source
> and stipulator of truth and the good, con-
> temporary thought reduces all reality to
> impersonal processes and events, and insists
> that man himself creatively imposes upon
> the cosmos and upon history the only values
> that they will ever bear.[15]

God is sovereign; He is the Lord of *whatever* and *all* in all of life. Thus, we must be cautious about our emphases. God changes things; we are His messengers. Our involvement is important, but we must remember that it is transitory. As beautiful and as meaningful as the works of humankind may be, they will not last. Theologian Karl Barth emphasized this by relating his comments to the tower of Babel: "In the building of the tower of Babel whose top is to touch heaven, the Church can have no part. The hope of the Church rests *on* God *for* men; it does not rest *on* men, not even on religious men—and not even on the belief that men *with the help of God* will finally build that tower."[16] Our hope is not found in human efforts. Our hope is found in God's provision for eternity. But this does not denigrate our involvement with culture. "There is a radical difference between human culture generally, which is thoroughly secular, and that which is developed as a loving service to God."[17] Utopia will never refer to this life. Because no culture "this side of the Parousia can be recognized as divine we are limited to the more modest hope that life on earth may gradually be made better; or, more modestly still, gradually be made less bad."[18] A Christian's response to culture should be described with such modest hopes in view.

This chapter has focused on five principles that can strengthen a Christian impact on culture. Fill your mind with biblical precepts; be careful that you don't respond to the surrounding world with cultural biases; be interactive but not accommodating; develop a positive, revolutionary mind-set; and glorify God in all of life.

2

Culture
and the Bible

Jerry Solomon

This is not a Christian culture. We are living in an environment that challenges us to evaluate continually what it means to live the Christian life. So how do we respond? The answer begins with the Bible. Our view of culture must include biblical insights. In this chapter we strive to investigate selected passages of Scripture pertaining to culture.

The Golden Calf and the Tabernacle: Judging Culture

Chapters 31–39 of Exodus provide a unique perspective of culture and God's involvement with it. On one hand, human work was blessed through the artistry of Bezalel, Oholiab, and other skilled artisans as they cooperated to build the tabernacle (chaps. 35–39). On the other hand, God rejected human work in the form of the golden calf (chaps. 31–34). This contrast serves to suggest a guideline by which we can begin to judge culture.

Chapter 31:1–11 contains God's initial instructions to Moses concerning the building of the tabernacle in the wilderness. God recognized two important artisans, Bezalel and Oholiab, as being especially gifted for this work. These men were skilled, creative people who were able to contribute significantly to the religious/cultural life of the nation of Israel.[1] But at this point in the narrative, the scene changes dramatically.

While Moses was on the mountain with God, the people became impatient and decided to make a god, an idol. This decision prompted an enraged response from both God and Moses. The end result was tragic: Three thousand Israelites were slain as a result of their idolatry.

Then the attention of the people was directed toward the building of the tabernacle. Chapters 35–39 contain detailed accounts from God pertaining to the tabernacle and the subsequent work of the skilled artisans, including Bezalel and Oholiab. The finished product was blessed (39:42–43).

In this brief survey of a portion of Israel's history, we see two responses to the work of human hands, one negative and the other positive. The people fashioned a piece of art, an idol; the response was negative on the part of God and Moses. The people fashioned another piece of art, the tabernacle; the response was positive and worthy of the blessing of both God and Moses. Why the difference in judgment? The answer is deceptively simple: the intent of the art was evaluated. And it was not a matter of one being "secular" and the other "sacred." Art, the cultural product, was not the problem. "Just as art can be used in the name of the true God, as shown in the gifts of Bezalel, so it can be used in an idolatrous way, supplanting the place of God and thereby distorting its own nature."[2]

Art is certainly a vital element of culture. As a result, we should take to heart the lessons of Exodus 31–39. Our evaluation of culture should include an awareness of intent without being overly sensitive to form. If not, we begin to assign evil incorrectly. As Carl F. H. Henry says, "The world is evil only as a fallen world. It is not evil intrinsically."[3]

These insights have focused on certain observers of cultural objects: God, Moses, and the people of Israel. In the first case God and Moses saw the golden calf from one perspective, but the people of Israel saw it from another perspective. In the second case, all of them were in agreement as they observed the tabernacle. The people's perception changed; they agreed with God's intent and aesthetic judgment. The lesson is that our cultural life is subject to God.

Entering the Fray

How do you react when you're out of your comfort zone—away from your surroundings, friends, and family? Do you cringe and disengage yourself? Or do you boldly make the best of the new situation?

The first chapter of Daniel tells of four young men who were transported by a conquering nation, Babylon, to a culture other than their own. Their response to this condition provides us with insights concerning how we should relate to the culture that surrounds us. Daniel, of course, proves to be the central figure among the four. He is the focus of our attention.

Note the following facets of this chapter.

1. Daniel and his friends were chosen by the king of Babylon, Nebuchadnezzar, to serve in his court. They were chosen because of their "intelligence in every branch of wisdom . . . understanding . . . discerning knowledge, and . . . ability for serving in the king's court" (v. 4).

2. They were taught "the literature and language of the Chaldeans" (v. 4).
3. Daniel "made up his mind" that he would not partake of the Babylonian food and drink (v. 8).
4. "God granted Daniel favor and compassion" with his superiors even though he and his friends would not partake of the food (vv. 9–16).
5. "God gave them knowledge and intelligence in every branch of literature and wisdom" (v. 17).
6. The king found Daniel and his friends to be "ten times better than all the magicians and conjurers who were in all his realm" (v. 20).

This synopsis provides us with several important observations. First, Daniel and his friends made no attempt to separate themselves totally from the culture, in particular from the educational system of that culture. This was a typical response among the ancient Jews. These young men were capable of interacting with an ungodly culture without being contaminated by it. Evangelicals are often paranoid about living within what is deemed a non-Christian culture. Perhaps we can learn a lesson from Daniel concerning a proper response. Of course, such a response should be based on wisdom and discernment.

Second, even though Daniel and his companions learned from the culture, they did so by practicing discernment. They obviously compared what they learned of Babylonian thought with what they already understood from God's point of view. The Law of God was something with which they were well acquainted. Edward Young's comments on Daniel 1:17 clarify this point: "The knowledge and intelligence which God gave to them . . . was of a discerning kind, that they might know and possess the ability to accept what was true and to reject what was false in their instruction."[4] Such perception is greatly needed among evangelicals. A separatist, isolationist mentality creates moral and spiritual vacuums throughout our culture. We should replace those vacuums with ideas that are spawned in the minds of godly thinkers and doers.

Third, God approved of their condition within the culture and even gave them what was needed to influence it (v. 17). God might direct evangelicals to enter a foreign culture that does not share their worldview. Or He might direct them to enter the culture that surrounds them, which, as with contemporary Western culture, can be devoid of the overt influence of a Christian worldview. If so, they should do so with an understanding that the Lord will protect them and provide for them. And He will demonstrate His power through them as the surrounding culture responds to them.

"The World" in the New Testament

In and *of* are two simple words that can stimulate a lot of thought when it comes to what the Bible says about culture or the world. After all, we are to be *in* the world but not *of* it. Let's see what the New Testament has to say.

The terms *kosmos* and *aiōn,* both of which are generally translated "world," are employed numerous times in the New Testament. A survey of *kosmos* will provide important insights. George Eldon Ladd explains the use of the word.[5]

First, the world can refer to "both the entire created order (John 17:5, 24) and the earth in particular (John 11:9; 16:21; 21:25)."[6] This means that "there is no trace of the idea that there is anything evil about the world."[7]

Second, *"kosmos* can designate not only the world but also those who inhabit the world: mankind (John 12:19; 18:20; 7:4; 14:22)."[8] Third, "the most interesting use of *kosmos* . . . is found in the sayings where the world—mankind—is the object of God's love and salvation."[9]

But people, in addition to being the objects of God's love, are seen "as sinful, rebellious, and alienated from God, as fallen humanity. The *kosmos* is characterized by wickedness (John 7:7), and does not know God (John 17:25) nor his emissary, Christ (John 1:10)."[10] "Again and again . . . the world is presented as something hostile to God."[11] But Ladd reminds us that "what makes the *kosmos* evil is not something intrinsic to it, but the fact that it has turned away from its creator and has become enslaved to evil powers."[12]

So what is the Christian's responsibility in this evil, rebellious world? "The disciples' reaction is not to be one of withdrawal from the world, but of living in the world, motivated by the love of God rather than the love of the world."[13] "So his followers are not to find their security and satisfaction on the human level as does the world, but in devotion to the redemptive purpose of God" (John 17:17, 19).[14]

The apostle Paul related that "'worldliness' consists of worshipping the creature rather than the creator (Rom. 1:25), of finding one's pride and glory on the human and created level rather than in God. The world is sinful only insofar as it exalts itself above God and refuses to humble itself and acknowledge its creative Lord."[15] The world is seen as it should be seen when we first worship its Creator.

This summary of *kosmos* contributes the following points that can be applied to our survey.

1. The world is hostile toward God; this includes the rebellion of humankind.

2. This hostility was not part of the original created order; the world was created good.
3. This world is also the object of God's redemptive love and Christ's sacrifice.
4. The world is not to be seen as an end in itself. We are always to view culture in the light of eternity.
5. We are to be about the business of transforming the world. "We are not to follow the world's lead but to cut across it and rise above it to a higher calling and style."[16] Or, as Ronald Allen says, "Ours is a world of lechery and war. It is also a world of the good, the beautiful, and the lovely. Eschew lechery; embrace the lovely—and live for the praise of God in the only world we have!"[17]

We need a balance that does not reject beauty but at the same time recognizes the ugly. Our theology should entail both, and the world needs to see this.

Corinthians and Culture

"You're a Corinthian!" If you had heard that exclamation in New Testament times, you would know that the person who said it was very upset. To call someone a Corinthian was insulting. Even non-Christians recognized that Corinth was one of the most immoral cities in the known world.

Paul's first letter to the Corinthians contains many indications of this situation. The believers in Corinth were faced with a culture that resembled ours in several ways. It was diverse ethnically, religiously, and philosophically. It was a center of wealth, literature, and the arts. And it was infamous for its blatant sexual immorality. How would Paul advise believers to respond to life in such a city?

That question can be answered by concentrating on several principles that can be discovered in Paul's letter. We will highlight only a few of these principles by focusing on certain terms.

Liberty is a foundational term for Christians entering the culture, but it can be misunderstood easily because some people act as if it implies total freedom. But "the believer's life is one of Christian liberty in grace."[18] Paul wrote, "All things are lawful for me, but not all things are profitable. All things are lawful for me, but I will not be mastered by anything" (6:12; 10:23). We must remember, though, that this liberty is given to glorify God. A liberty that condones sin is another form of slavery. Thus, "Whether . . . you eat or drink or whatever you do, do all to the glory of God" (10:31). In addition, we must be aware of how unbelievers view our liberty. Again Paul wrote, "Give no offense either to Jews or to Greeks or to the church of God" (10:32).

Conscience is another term that figures prominently in how we enter the culture. We must be very sensitive to what it means to defile the conscience. We must be sensitive to what tempts us. "The believer who cannot visit the world without making it his home has no right to visit at his weak points."[19] As a result, we need to cultivate the necessary discipline to respond to the ways the Spirit speaks through our conscience.

Yet another term is *brother*. In particular, we should beware of becoming a "stumbling block" to the person Paul calls a "weaker brother." This does not mean that we disregard what has been said about liberty. "A Christian need not allow his liberty to be curtailed by somebody else. But he is obliged to take care that that other person does not fall into sin and if he would hurt that person's conscience he has not fulfilled that obligation."[20] This requires a special sensitivity to others, which is a hallmark of the Christian life.

On many occasions, the Probe staff has experienced the challenge of applying these principles. For example, some of us speak frequently in a club in an area of Dallas, Texas, called "Deep Ellum." The particular club in which we teach includes a bar, a concert stage, and other things normally associated with such a place. Some people refer to the clientele as "nonconformists." We can use our liberty to minister in the club, but we must do so with a keen awareness of the principles we have discussed. When we enter that culture, which is so different from what we normally experience, we must do so by applying the wisdom found in God's Word to the Corinthians.

Encountering the World

How do you get a hearing when you have something to say? In particular, how do you share the truth of God in ungodly surroundings?

Paul's encounter with Athenian culture (Acts 17:16–34) is illustrative of the manner in which we can converse with contemporary culture. His interaction exhibits an ability to communicate with a diversity of the population, from those in the marketplace to the Epicurean and Stoic philosophers. And he exhibits an understanding of the culture, including its literature and art. Paul was giving a model for relating our faith effectively. That is, we must communicate with language and examples that our audience can understand.

Verse 16 says that Paul's "spirit was being provoked within him as he was beholding the city full of idols." Note that the verb translated "provoked" here is the Greek word from which we derive the term *paroxysm*. Paul was highly irritated. In addition, note that the Greek verb form is imperfect passive, implying that his agitation was a logical result of his Christian conscience, and that it was continuous. The idolatry that permeated Athenian culture stimulated this dramatic response. *Application:* The idolatry of contemporary culture should bring no less a response from us. Examples of ideologies that have become idols in our culture are materialism, individualism, relativism, and secularism.

Verses 17 and 18 refer to several societal groups: Jews, God-fearing Gentiles, Epicurean and Stoic philosophers, as well as the general population, namely, "those who happened to be present." Evidently, Paul was able to converse with any segment of the population. *Application:* As alert, thinking, sensitive, concerned, discerning Christians, we are challenged to confront our culture in all of its variety and pluralism. It is easier to converse with those who are like-minded, but that is not our only responsibility.

In verse 18 some of the philosophers call Paul an "idle babbler" (i.e., one who makes his living by picking up scraps). *Application:* We should realize that the Christian worldview, in particular the basic tenets of the gospel, will often elicit scorn from a culture that is too often foreign to Christian truth. This reaction, however, should not hinder us from sharing the truth.

The narrative of verses 19–31 indicates that Paul knew enough about Athenian culture to converse with the Athenians on the highest intellectual level. He was acutely aware of the "points of understanding" between him and his audience. He was also acutely aware of the "points of disagreement" and did not hesitate to stress them. He had enough knowledge of their literary expressions to quote their spokesmen (i.e., their poets), even though this does not necessarily mean that Paul had a thorough knowledge of them. And he called them to repentance. *Application:* We should "stretch" ourselves more intellectually so that we can duplicate Paul's experience more frequently. The most influential seats in our culture too often are left to those who are devoid of Christian thought. Such a condition is in urgent need of change.

Paul experienced three reactions in Athens (vv. 32–34).

1. "Some began to sneer" (v. 32). They expressed contempt.
2. Some said, "We shall hear you again concerning this" (v. 32).
3. "Some men joined him and believed" (v. 34).

We should not be surprised when God's message is rejected, we should be prepared when people want to hear more, and we can rejoice when the message falls on fertile soil and bears the fruit of a changed life.

Conclusion

We have seen that Scripture is not silent regarding culture. It contains much cultural information by way of example and precept, and we have only begun the investigation. There is more to be done. With this expectation in mind, what have we discovered from the Bible at this stage?

1. In some measure, God "is responsible for the presence of culture, for he created human beings such that they are culture-producing beings."[21]

2. God holds us responsible for cultural stewardship.
3. We should not fear the surrounding culture; instead, we should strive to contribute to it through God-given creativity and transform it through dialogue and proclamation.
4. We should practice discernment while living within culture.
5. The products of culture should be judged on the basis of intent, not form.

We advance the theory that God's basic attitude toward culture is that which the apostle Paul articulates in 1 Corinthians 9:19–22. That is, He views human culture primarily as a vehicle to be used by Him and His people for Christian purposes, rather than as an enemy to be combated or shunned.[22] Let us use the vehicle of culture for the glory of God!

3

Culture Wars

Don Closson

Americans are highly polarized when it comes to issues of morality and social norms. We feel our collective blood pressure rise as we read the daily newspaper or watch the news on television. We all feel the tension caused by problems such as teenage pregnancies, abortion, crime, poverty, and political corruption. Factions from across the political spectrum propose social programs and ideals that, they believe, would make America a better place for all to live. However, the problem is that these programs or ideals are often in direct conflict with each other and are often built upon very different assumptions about human nature. To highlight these differences, consider the following events.

In the early 1990s, members of the American Civil Liberties Union (ACLU) informed the Education Committee in the California State Assembly that they were opposed to a bill the committee was considering. The bill, which called for traditional values in school curricula, was offensive to the ACLU because it would mandate that students be taught that monogamous, heterosexual relations solely within marriage is a traditional American value. The ACLU argued that this would be an "unconstitutional establishment of a religious doctrine in public schools."[1] They contended that the bill was an obvious violation of the First Amendment.

A private school in Georgia asked a student either to change his behavior or leave the school. This in itself is not an unusual event. However, the student wasn't a discipline problem, and he wasn't failing academically. In fact, he was popular and liked by many people on campus. The problem was that he was cross-dressing. He dressed and behaved as a woman and was accepted by many students as a female. When the student chose to leave the school instead of change his attire, the school's drama teacher remarked, "I really think that we all lost something precious that night."[2]

To many Americans, the ACLU's action in the first incident is incomprehensible. It seems reasonable, healthy, and obvious for schools to implement a "traditional values" model for sex education. Those who side with the ACLU, however, find it just as incomprehensible that anyone would see their position as unreasonable or unusual. Some people might find the expulsion of the cross-dressing student in the second incident to be grossly unfair, whereas most parents would wonder why the school took so long to act.

Regardless of our perspective on these issues, we all agree that Americans find themselves with deep differences on a number of fundamental issues that govern our daily lives. Unfortunately, these deep differences have led some Americans to bomb a government building, shoot abortion doctors, and burn down a mountaintop ski resort to further their causes.

Although few Christians fail to see the conflict in our society, particularly in our schools, we are far from united as to what our response should be. However, from a historical perspective, times of cultural disruption are often times of great opportunity for the church—if it is all that God desires it to be.

In this chapter we will spotlight this culture war in which we find ourselves and consider what a biblical response might be. Along the way, we will consider insights from two books that have caught the attention of the press and academic community. The first book is William Bennett's *The De-Valuing of America*. Bennett is a former Secretary of Education in the Reagan administration and an astute cultural critic. The second book is *Culture Wars: The Struggle to Define America* by James Davison Hunter. This professor of sociology at the University of Virginia helps to frame the issue and offers some interesting examples of the conflict.

Orthodox Versus Progressive

Leaders of all political persuasions have noted the culture war that is engulfing our nation. Bennett argues that the battle over our culture is being fought between what he calls the liberal elite and the rest of society. The elite are "found among academics and intellectuals, in the literary world, in journals of political opinion, in Hollywood, in the artistic community, in mainline religious institutions, and in some quarters of the media."[3] He believes they are more powerful than their numbers would normally allow because they are looked upon as trendsetters and opinion makers. Differing from traditional elite groups in American history, these people reject the traditional bourgeois emphasis on "work, frugality, sexual restraint, and self-control."[4] As evidence of the existence of this elite he refers to studies by Stanley Rothman with Robert and Linda Richter. Their work portrays a media aristocracy that votes as a block for liberal candidates and for issues such as abortion, gay rights, and the environment.[5]

Bennett adds that this elite is marked by a wholesale rejection of American ideals, a calling into question of what has been known as the American dream.[6] Evidence is not as significant as ideology for the elite. Their approach is "one of vindication, not investigation."[7] If the middle class and the Republicans are for something, this group will instinctively be against it.

Hunter's approach to defining the warring camps is subtler and, I believe, more accurate. He believes that there is an elite on both sides of the culture war. On the one hand is what he calls the "orthodox" group. They have a commitment to an external, definable, and transcendent authority. From an evangelical perspective, this is the God of the Bible. God is a consistent and unchangeable measure of value, purpose, goodness, and identity. Hunter would also include in this group Jews and others who hold to a definable, unchanging, absolute authority.

Opposing this group are the "progressives." Progressives are distinguished by their ideals of modernism, rationalism, and subjectivism. To these people truth is more a process than a constant authority. It is an unfolding reality rather than an unchanging revelation. What is interesting about the progressives is that they often hold onto the religious heritage of the orthodox but reinterpret its meaning for modern consumption. For instance, to a gay progressive, Christ came not to free us from the penalty of sin but to free gays from the constraints of society. Although many progressives discard religion altogether, those who do claim the Christian tradition have usually adopted a liberation theology, liberating the individual from any obligation other than to love each other in a very vague sense. To love each other seems to mean to let people do whatever is expedient in their lives.

The real difference between the orthodox and the progressives is at the faith level. Whether people call themselves Christians is not nearly as important as the kind of reality in which they place their faith. Hunter believes that the culture war is a war of worldviews, and that these worldviews cause us to see the world differently. How, then, should Christians, those who place their faith in the sacrificial death of Christ as an atoning payment for their sins, respond to this culture war?

The Angry Christian

Unfortunately, in the eyes of the secular world Christians are often seen as angry, red-faced people. At school board meetings, abortion clinics, and even the funeral of a homosexual who was murdered because of his lifestyle, Christians are there to condemn sin and its perpetrators angrily. It is almost as if Christians are surprised by sin and feel that their only response is to point people to the law of God. As a result, many people outside the church see Christianity as a religion of law, similar to most other world religions. This is a tragedy.

Although the reaction is understandable, I don't believe that we as Christians are called to respond in anger to the culture war, especially not with anger directed at people. Although the wrath of God is evident in both the Old and the New Testaments, condemnation of human anger is also present in each. Near the very beginning of human culture, God warns Cain about his anger and downcast face. Instead of seeking to do what was right, Cain was angry with God and his situation (Gen. 4:6–7). The wisdom literature of Proverbs reminds us, "A gentle answer turns away wrath, but a harsh word stirs up anger," and "A quick-tempered man does foolish things, and a crafty man is hated" (Prov. 15:1; 14:17 NIV).

In the New Testament, Paul condemns "hatred," and "fits of rage" immediately before listing the spiritual fruit of love, joy, peace, patience, kindness, goodness, faithfulness, gentleness, and self-control (Gal. 5:22–23). James 1:19–20 is fairly straightforward in maintaining, "Everyone should be quick to listen, slow to speak and slow to become angry, for man's anger does not bring about the righteous life that God desires" (NIV). Jesus set an extraordinarily high standard against anger and hatred in His Sermon on the Mount. He taught, "You have heard that it was said to the people long ago, 'Do not murder, and anyone who murders will be subject to judgment.' But I tell you that anyone who is angry with his brother will be subject to judgment" (Matt. 5:21–22 NIV). Jesus is speaking about the root cause of much evil in any society: an angry, unforgiving heart.

Some people may respond that righteous indignation, or anger against sin, is merely emulating Christ. After all, Jesus cleared the Temple with a whip and violently over-turned the moneylenders' tables. Are we not allowed the same righteous indignation? I think not, especially if we take seriously God's admonition to let Him be in charge of judgment and vengeance (Rom. 12:19). In fact, Paul tells us to feed our enemy if he is hungry, to give him drink if he is thirsty, and to overcome evil by doing good (Rom. 12:20–21). The difference between Jesus' righteous indignation and our anger is that Jesus, being God, has the right to judge, and, being perfectly righteous, His judgment is perfect. He knows the hearts of men and has no bias other than holiness itself. On the other hand, we are often most angry when our personal comfort is disturbed. To the watching world, Christians become most interested in politics when their personal wealth or comfort is at stake.

I don't believe that God is calling His people to anger in America. We bring a message of grace to the lost, not a message of law.

Apathy

Many Christians have been active in the culture war since the early 1980s. With the rise of conservative politics and the family values movement, Christians joined the Republican Party in droves and joined numerous other organizations to help fight against the moral decline of the nation. Given what appears, in many ways, to be a rejection of the conservative moral agenda in contemporary American life, it is tempting for many people simply to retreat from activism altogether.

Some Christians never did get engaged in a countercultural sense. In fact, an early evangelical leader in culture war activity, Francis Schaeffer, warned that most Christians were more concerned with personal peace and affluence than about having an impact on their society.[8] He was concerned that as the Christian-dominated consensus weakened, these two values would grow in their place. The picture of society with which we are left is one in which people's lives are consumed by things—buying two sport-utility vehicles and a nice big house in the suburbs, with a nice tall fence, a color TV, and a remote control. These people do not want to know about the suffering in our urban ghettos or about the plight of Christians in other countries. They want their lives to be unimpeded by the turmoil experienced by less affluent people.

Is it wrong to have a nice house and cars? No, it isn't. But neither is this the purpose for which our Lord has called us. Gathering nice things should not drive our daily activities. When Jesus was asked what the greatest commandments were, He responded that we are first to love God with all our heart, soul, and mind (Matt. 22:37), and second to love our neighbor as ourselves. Christians should measure success in this life against these two goals. The rest of revelation, both the written Word and the life of Christ, gives us a picture of what this means in both the general culture and within the Church. Christ gave us the Great Commission, to go into all nations, making disciples and teaching what He taught (Matt. 28:19–20). Paul wrote about our being living sacrifices with renewed minds that can know the will of God for ourselves (Rom. 12:1–2).

To be indifferent to sin is not to love God; this form of apathy is incompatible with true Christian faith. However, to be indifferent to suffering in the world is equally incompatible with our faith. Ignoring oppression and hatred reveals a lack of love for our neighbors. Too often Christians seem to get excited only when their rights, whether property or religious, are threatened. This attitude makes a mockery of our Lord's words: "A new command I give you: Love one another. As I have loved you, so you must love one another. By this all men will know that you are my disciples, if you love one another" (John 13:34–35). In Romans 12, Paul wrote about blessing those who persecute you, and if it is possible, to be at peace with everyone around you.

Hebrews 12 tells us to throw off everything that entangles

us, everything that keeps us from running the race that Jesus marked out for us. We are to fix our eyes on Him, who endured the cross because its joyous result would be a redeemed people of God.

Ambassadors for Christ

When we are thinking about how to respond to the culture war in America, or in any culture, we must ask ourselves what we are trying to accomplish. In the language of real war, what are our tactical and strategic goals? Some people might respond that we are here to fight sin, to rid our society of the evils of abortion, homosexuality, adultery, drug abuse, political corruption, and so on. Some Christians claim that our primary cultural objective is to reinstate Mosaic Law by taking control of the government and using its legal authority to impose a moral society on the population. However, this does not appear to be the plan revealed to us in the New Testament.

In 2 Corinthians 5, Paul details the role we are to play in America (or in any country in which we might live). We are to be Christ's ambassadors, and our message is one of reconciliation with God. Many religions teach a message of law: Islam, Judaism, and most Eastern religions focus on the works people must do to please God or the gods. They focus on how humanity must reform itself to gain God's favor. Christianity's message is *grace,* and as Christ's ambassadors we proclaim that God has reconciled Himself to us in Christ by making "him who had no sin to be sin for us, so that in him we might become the righteousness of God" (2 Cor. 5:21). God is making the righteousness of Christ available to sinners; salvation is the crediting of Christ's righteousness to our personal account, thus satisfying the judgment of a holy God against our personal sins.

What about social activism? What about politics? Do we just share the gospel and ignore the problems facing our nation? No, we are to be salt and light in a decaying world. However, our trust is not in politics, which can change only a nation's laws and, to a lesser degree, its people's behavior. Even if abortion ended tomorrow, if every homosexual became heterosexual, and if drugs and pornography were things of the past, people would still be lost in their sins.

The role of an ambassador is complex. Ambassadors must be intimately familiar with the nature of their sovereign's kingdom. All Christians must seek to know God and His message in a way that can be communicated to the culture in which they live. Unfortunately, Christians often know the message but have a difficult time communicating it so that the surrounding culture understands it and in a way that answers the questions that society is asking. Stating the gospel accurately and meaningfully is central to being an effective ambassador for Christ.

If we are to respond to the culture war by being ambassadors for Christ, then keeping the church vital becomes far more important than controlling the White House or Congress. And understanding how to communicate the gospel of Christ is infinitely more valuable than having the most potent political strategy. Being faithful to Christ in this way builds God's kingdom on earth and results in common grace as more and more believers participate in every aspect of our culture.

4

Worldviews

Jerry Solomon

A friend of mine recently told me of a conversation he had with a good friend we will call Joe. Joe is a doctor. He is not a Christian. My friend was attempting to share Christ with Joe, but Joe was not responding. Therefore, my friend decided to change his approach. He said, "Joe, you're an excellent doctor. You care deeply about your patients. Why do you care so much for people since you believe we have evolved by chance? What gives us value?"

Joe was stunned by the question and couldn't answer it. He had never thought about it. Now he was more receptive to my friend's discussion of Christ. His "worldview" had taken a blow.

The concept of a worldview has received increasing attention over the past several years. Many books have been written on the subject of worldviews from both Christian and non-Christian perspectives. Frequently speakers will refer to the term. On occasion even reviews of movies and music will include the phrase. All of this attention prompts us to ask, "What does the term *worldview* mean?" and "What difference does it make?" Our intent is to answer these questions. As a result, we hope that all of us will give closer attention to both our own worldview and the worldviews of those around us.

What Is a Worldview?

What is a worldview? Numerous authors offer a variety of definitions. For example, James Sire asserts, "A worldview is a set of presuppositions (or assumptions) which we hold (consciously or subconsciously) about the basic makeup of our world."[1] Phillips and Brown state, "A worldview is, first of all, an explanation and interpretation of the world and second, an application of this view to life. In simpler terms, our worldview is a view of the world and a view for the world."[2] Walsh and Middleton, however, provide the most succinct and understandable explanation: "A worldview provides a model of the world which guides its adherents in the world."[3] With the realization that many subtleties can be added, theirs will be our working definition.

The Need for a Worldview

Worldviews act somewhat like eyeglasses or contact lenses. That is, a worldview should provide the correct "prescription" for making sense of the world just as wearing the correct prescription for your eyes brings things into focus. In either example, an incorrect prescription can be dangerous, even life-threatening. People who are struggling with worldview questions are often despairing and even suicidal; therefore, it's important for us to give attention to the formulation of the proper worldview.

Arthur Holmes states that the need for a worldview is fourfold: "the need to unify thought and life; the need to define the good life and find hope and meaning in life; the need to guide thought; the need to guide action."[4] Yet another prominent need for the proper worldview is to help us deal with an increasingly diverse culture. We are faced with a smorgasbord of worldviews, all of which make claims concerning truth. We are challenged to sort through this mixture of worldviews with wisdom. All people experience needs, either consciously or subconsciously. All of us have worldviews with which we strive to meet our needs. The proper worldview helps us by orienting us to the intellectual and philosophical terrain about us.

Worldviews are so much a part of our lives that we see and hear them daily, regardless of whether we recognize them. Movies, television, music, magazines, newspapers, government, education, science, art, and all other aspects of culture are affected by worldviews. We ignore their importance to our detriment. For example, consider the movies you have seen lately. Have you thought of the fact that the director behind the camera has a worldview that is transmitted through the lens of the camera? The director's worldview is being espoused as he leads us through the scenes that compose the plot of the story.

Testing Worldviews

A worldview should pass certain tests. First, it should be rational. It should not ask us to believe contradictory things. Second, it should be supported by evidence. It should be consistent with what we observe. Third, it should give a satisfying, comprehensive explanation of reality. It should be able to explain why things are the way they are. Fourth, it should provide a satisfactory basis for living. It should not leave us feeling compelled to borrow elements of another worldview to live in this world.

Components Found in All Worldviews

In addition to putting worldviews to these tests, we should also see that worldviews have the following four common components, and it is important to keep these in mind as you establish your own worldview and as you share it with others.

1. *Something exists.* This may sound obvious, but it really is an important foundational element of worldview building. Some people will try to deny it, but a denial is self-defeating. All people experience the principle of cause and effect. The universe is rational; it is predictable.

2. *All people have absolutes.* Again, many people will try to deny this point, but to deny it is to assert it. All of us seek an infinite reference point. For some people that point is God; for others it is the state, or love, or power; and for still others it is themselves or man.

3. *Two contradictory statements cannot both be correct.* This is a primary law of logic that many people attempt to deny. Ideally, only one worldview can correctly mirror reality. This fact cannot be overemphasized in light of the prominent belief that tolerance is the ultimate virtue. To say that someone is wrong is labeled intolerant or narrow-minded. A good illustration of this is when we hear people declare that all religions are the same. This statement would mean that Hindus, for example, agree with Christians concerning God, Jesus, salvation, heaven, hell, and a host of other doctrines. But such a view is nonsense.

4. *All people exercise faith.* All of us presuppose certain things to be true without tangible proof. These

presuppositions are inferences or assumptions upon which a belief is based. This point becomes important, for example, when we interact with those who allege that only the scientist is completely neutral. Some common assumptions are that a personal God exists, that man evolved from inorganic material, that man is essentially good, and that reality is material.

As we talk with people who have opposing worldviews, an understanding of these common components can help us listen more patiently, and it can guide us to make our case more wisely.

Six Worldview Questions

Have you ever been frustrated searching for ways to stir the thinking of a non-Christian friend? The following six questions are helpful with this task. They can stir your thinking about the subject of worldviews.[5] Each of them will be answered with various non-Christian responses. We will discuss Christian responses later in this chapter.

1. *Why is there something rather than nothing?* Some people may actually say that something came from nothing. Others may state that something is here because of an impersonal spirit or energy. And there are those who believe that matter is eternal.

2. *How do you know that you know?* Some people say that the mind is the center of our source of knowledge. Things are known only deductively. Other people claim that knowledge is found only in the senses; we know only what is perceived.

3. *How do you explain human nature?* Frequently people will say that we are born as blank slates, neither

good nor evil. Another popular response is that we are born good, but society causes us to behave otherwise.

4. *How do you determine what is right and wrong?* Often we hear it said that ethics are relative or situational. Others assert that we have no free choice because we are entirely determined. Some people simply derive "oughts" from what "is." And, of course, history has shown us the tragic results of a "might-makes-right" answer.

5. *What is the meaning of history?* One answer is that history is determined by a mechanistic universe. Another answer is that history is a linear stream of events linked by cause and effect but without purpose. Yet another answer is that history is meaningless because life is absurd.

6. *What happens to a person at death?* Many people will say that a person's death is just the disorganization of matter. Increasingly, people in our culture are saying that death brings reincarnation or realization of oneness.

Alert Christians will quickly recognize that the preceding answers are contrary to their beliefs and that the differences are definite and sometimes startling. Worldviews are in collision; therefore, we should know at least something about the worldviews that are central to the conflict. And we should certainly be able to articulate a Christian worldview.

Examples of Worldviews

In his excellent book *The Universe Next Door,* James Sire catalogs the most influential worldviews of the past and present: deism, nihilism, atheistic existentialism, Christian theism, naturalism, postmodernism, New Age, and Eastern pantheism.[6]

Deism, a prominent worldview during the eighteenth century, is no longer in vogue in the broad base of the population. The deist believes in a God who created and then abandoned the universe.

Nihilism, a more recent worldview, is alive among many young people and some intellectuals. Nihilists see no value to reality; life is absurd.

Atheistic existentialism is influential and can be seen frequently. The existentialist, like the nihilist, sees life as absurd, but also sees human beings as totally free to make their own meaning in the face of this absurdity.

Christian theism, naturalism, postmodernism, and *New Age* (closely related to Eastern pantheism) are now the most influential worldviews in the United States. We will survey each of them in the following paragraphs.

Christian Theism

Let's return to the six questions we asked earlier and briefly see how the Christian theist might answer them.

1. *Question:* Why is there something rather than nothing?
   Answer: There is an infinite-personal God who has created the universe out of nothing.
2. *Question:* How do you know that you know?
   Answer: Reason and experience can be legitimate teachers, but a transcendent source is necessary. We know some things only because God tells us through the Bible.
3. *Question:* How do you explain human nature?
   Answer: Man was originally created good in God's image, but he chose to sin, thus infecting all of

humanity with what is called a "sin nature." So man's Creator has endowed him with value, but his negative behavior is in league with his nature.

4. *Question:* How do you determine what is right and wrong?
   Answer: God reveals in the Bible the guidelines for our conduct.

5. *Question:* What is the meaning of history?
   Answer: History is a linear and meaningful sequence of events leading to the fulfillment of God's purposes for man.

6. *Question:* What happens to a person at death?
   Answer: Death is either the gate to life with God (heaven) or to eternal separation from Him (hell). The destination is dependent upon the response we give to God's provision for our sinfulness.

Christian theism has had a long history in Western culture. This does not mean that all individuals who have lived in Western culture have been Christians. It simply means that this worldview used to be dominant; it was the most influential worldview. This fact was true even among non-Christians; however, this is no longer valid. Western culture has experienced a transition to what is called naturalism.

Naturalism

Even though naturalism in various forms is ancient, we will use the term to refer to a worldview that has had considerable influence in a relatively short time within Western culture. The seeds were planted in the seventeenth century and began to flower in the eighteenth century.

Most of us have been exposed to naturalism through what is called secular humanism.

What are the basic tenets of this worldview? First, God is irrelevant. This tenet helps us better understand the term *naturalism;* it is in direct contrast to Christian theism, which is based on supernaturalism. Second, progress and evolutionary change are inevitable. Third, human beings are autonomous and self-centered and will save themselves. Fourth, education is the guide to life; intelligence and freedom guarantee full human potential. Fifth, science is the ultimate provider for both knowledge and morals. These principles have permeated our lives. In fact, they formed the foundation of the education of most of the populations of Western countries. They are also apparent, for example, in the media and government. We should be alert constantly to their influence.

Postmodernism

After World War II, postmodernism began to replace the confidence of naturalism. With it came the conclusion that truth, in any real sense, doesn't exist. This view may be the next major worldview, or anti-worldview, that will infect the culture. It is now the rage on many of our college campuses. In the meantime, though, the past few decades have brought us another ancient worldview dressed in Western clothing.

New Age

Various forms of pantheism have been prominent in Eastern cultures for thousands of years, but they began to have an effect on Western culture in the 1950s. Various attempts had been made to introduce pantheistic teachings before then, but those attempts did not arouse the interest that was stirred in that decade. These teachings are now most readily observed in what is called the New Age movement. We could call it "Westernized Easternism," in that the ideas of the ancient east have been put in a Western context.

What are the basic tenets of this worldview? First, all is one. There are no ultimate distinctions between humans, animals, or the rest of creation. Second, since all is one, all is god. All of life has a spark of divinity. Third, if all is one and all is god, then each of us is god. Fourth, humans must discover their own divinity by experiencing a change in consciousness. We suffer from a collective form of metaphysical amnesia. Fifth, humans travel through indefinite cycles of birth, death, and reincarnation to work off what is called "bad karma." Sixth, New Age disciples think in terms of gray, not black and white. Thus they believe that two conflicting statements can both be true.

On the popular level these tenets are asserted through the media, including books, magazines, television, and movies. Perhaps the most visible teachers are Shirley MacLaine and Deepak Chopra. But these beliefs are also found increasingly among intellectuals in fields such as medicine, psychology, sociology, and education.

Conclusion

We have scanned the subject of worldviews very briefly. Let's return to the definition we affirmed in the beginning of this chapter: "A worldview provides a model of the world which guides its adherents in the world." If your model of the world includes an infinite, personal God, as in Christian theism, that belief should provide guidance for your life. If your model rejects God, as in naturalism, again such a belief serves as a guide. If your model rejects the possibility of truth, as in postmodernism, the implications should be obvious. Or if your model asserts that you are god, as in the New Age movement, yet again your life is being guided by such a conception. These examples should remind us that we are living in a culture that puts us in touch constantly with these and other ideas. They cannot all be true.

Thus, some of us may be confronted with the need to think more deeply than ever before. Some of us may need to purge from our lives those things that are contrary to Christian theism. Some of us may need to understand better that our thoughts are to be unified with daily life. Some of us may need to better understand that the good life and hope and meaning are found only through God's answers. Some of us may need to let God's ideas guide our thoughts more completely. And some of us may need to let God's guidelines guide our actions more fully.

Paul's admonition to the believers in ancient Colossae couldn't be more contemporary or helpful in light of our discussion:

> See to it that no one takes you captive through philosophy and empty deception [or worldviews], according to the tradition of men, according to the elementary principles of the world, rather than according to Christ. (Col. 2:8)

5

The Christian Mind

Jerry Solomon

Repent, for the kingdom of heaven is at hand.
(Matt. 4:17)

This familiar admonition was first spoken by John the Baptist and soon after it was echoed by Jesus.[1] The phrase certainly is worthy of a great deal of attention; it provides a lot of "food for thought." For the moment, though, let's concentrate on the first word: *Repent.*

This expression is central to the doctrines concerning sin and salvation. Literally it refers to a "change of mind." It doesn't mean that one is to be sorry for some action. Thus, the first hearers were admonished to realize that they were in need of radical change before a holy God, beginning with their minds. They were to turn from sin to God by changing their thinking.

Certainly the same need holds true for us. Most of us are in need of reminders that lead us back to one of the crucial aspects of our salvation: repentance, or a change in our thinking. In addition, we should couple such reminders with the realization that our changed minds should always be alive to God. To paraphrase Kepler's famous phrase, we are to "think God's thoughts after Him." Since the Christian life is all-inclusive, the mind is included.

"But," some people may ask, "do we actually have a mind?" Current research and thought in the fields of neuroscience and evolutionary psychology conclude that we are much too free with the word *mind.* Perhaps we should get used to referring to the brain, not to the mind. "Some neuroscientists are beginning to suspect that everything that makes people human is no more than an interaction of chemicals and electricity inside the labyrinthine folds of the brain."[2]

E. O. Wilson, the father of what is called sociobiology, proposes that we can determine an ethical system based on scientifically observable evidence.[3] He writes, "The empiricist argument holds that if we explore the biological roots of moral behavior, and explain their material origins and biases, we should be able to fashion a wise and enduring ethical consensus."[4] Thus, ethics are not to be found external to physical reality; there is no mind through which we can respond ethically. It seems that Wilson and likeminded people believe that "the mind is headed for an ignoble fate. Just as the twinkle of stars was reduced to nuclear explosions, and life itself to biochemical reactions, so the brain may one day be explained by the same forces that run the rest of the universe."[5]

Such perspectives should come as no surprise if we are aware of the permeation of a naturalistic worldview in both the physical and the social sciences. The Christian, though, is not relegated to this type of reduction. A biblical worldview makes clear that we are more than physical beings; we are also nonphysical beings made in God's image. As a popular joke from the nineteenth century said,

What is matter?—Never mind.
What is mind?—No matter.[6]

The truth of the joke should not be lost on those of us who claim to be followers of Christ. We should realize the importance of cultivating Christian minds. As the great statesman Charles Malik stated, "As Christ is the Light of the World, his light must shine and be brought to bear upon the problem of the formation of the mind."[7]

The Scriptures and the Mind (Part 1)

"Come now, and let us reason together," says the LORD.
(Isa. 1:18)

Imagine that you are in a courtroom. You are the defense attorney; the prosecutor is God Himself. He has just invited you, as Judah's attorney, to engage in debate concerning the case at hand, which happens to focus on the crimes of your client. Indeed, He wants the two of you to *reason together.* That is the scenario presented in this famous passage from the first chapter of Isaiah. God was inviting Judah to debate a case in court.[8] What a remarkable idea! And what a stunning statement concerning the importance of the mind. God was calling upon His people to use their minds to see if they could engage Him in debate concerning their sins.

In a time when the mind appears to be denigrated at every hand, such a passage should serve to reawaken us to the importance of using the minds God has given us. After all, the Bible, which most Christians claim to be the very Word of God, calls the mind to attention throughout its pages. As J. P. Moreland states, "If we are going to be wise, spiritual people prepared to meet the crises of our age, we must be a studying, learning community that values the life of the mind."[9] Let's begin such studying and learning by considering some of what the Bible says about, first, the ungodly and rebellious mind and, then, the godly mind.

The ungodly mind is described in terms that are sobering, to say the least. When we apply these phrases to the culture around us, we can better understand why what we see and hear disturbs us. For example, Romans 1:18–28 describes what one scholar called "The Night." Here are some of the ways this dark passage depicts unbelievers' minds:

- suppressing the truth
- rejecting God
- foolish speculations
- foolish hearts
- professing wisdom
- exchanging God for a counterfeit
- lusting hearts
- exchanging truth for a lie
- worshiping the creature
- degrading passions
- exchanging the natural for the unnatural
- committing indecent acts
- depraved minds

Another somber statement about the ungodly way of thinking is found in 2 Corinthians 4:4: "The god of this world has blinded the minds of the unbelieving so that they might not see the light of the gospel of the glory of Christ, who is the image of God." Perhaps you have had conversations with unbelievers that were characteristic of such "blindness." The person with whom you were talking just didn't "get it" as you attempted to share the truth of Christ. Such a response should not surprise us.

The Scriptures also frequently describe a foolish mind. Jeremiah 4:22 is a strong indictment of those who know the things of God but foolishly reject them: "For My people are foolish, they know Me not; they are stupid children and have no understanding. They are shrewd to do evil, but to do good they do not know." Hosea 4:6 shows the result of God's reaction when His people reject the truth: "My people are destroyed for lack of knowledge. Because you have rejected knowledge, I also will reject you from being My priest."

These ancient proclamations couldn't be more contemporary. May we heed their warnings!

The Scriptures and the Mind (Part 2)

We are destroying speculations and every lofty
thing raised up against the knowledge of God,
and we are taking every thought captive to the
obedience of Christ.
(2 Cor. 10:5)

When the apostle Paul wrote these words, he was very aware of the need for a Christian mind. Philosophical speculations abounded in his time, just as they do in our time. Thus, he described the Christian's mental responsibility in terms of warfare. The Christian mind is active —it enters the battle; it is filled with the knowledge of God—it is prepared for battle; it puts all things under the lordship of Christ—it follows the only true commander into battle. And that battle has been won innumerable times, even in the minds of brilliant people. "One of the most astonishing and undeniable arguments for the truth of [Christianity] is the fact that some of the most subtle of human intellects have been led to render submission to the Saviour."[10] The Bible contains many such insights into the nature of a Christian mind, but we will consider two of them.

Reason is a term that is descriptive of the Christian mind. This doesn't mean that Christians are to be rationalists, but they are to use reason based on the reason of God found in Scripture. For example, on one of several occasions Pharisees and Sadducees came to Jesus to test Him by asking for a sign from heaven. Jesus responded by referring to their ability to discern signs of certain kinds of weather. Then He asked, "Do you know how to discern the appearance of the sky, but cannot discern the signs of the times?" (Matt 16:3). Obviously He was noting how people use reason to arrive at conclusions, but the Christian mind would conclude the things of God.

The book of Acts indicates that the apostle Paul used reason consistently to persuade his hearers of the truth of his message. Acts 17:2–3 states that "according to Paul's custom, he went to them, and for three Sabbaths *reasoned* with them from the Scriptures, explaining and giving evidence that the Christ had to suffer and rise again from the dead" (emphasis added). For two years in Ephesus, Paul "was *reasoning* daily in the school of Tyrannus" (Acts 19:9, emphasis added). In light of the fact that our contemporary world attempts to reject reason, such examples should spur us to "hold out" for the possibility of reasonable dialogue with those around us. After all, those who reject reason must use reason to reject reason.

If the Christian mind is characterized by reason, such reason must be founded upon knowledge from God. Upon reflection of their conversation with Jesus on the road to Emmaus, two of the disciples said, "Were not our hearts burning within us while He was speaking to us on the road, while He was explaining the Scriptures to us?" (Luke 24:32). The word *hearts* in this passage refers to both moral and mental perception. In his letter to the Colossians Paul wrote, "We proclaim Him, admonishing every man and teaching every man with all wisdom, that we may present every man complete in Christ" (Col. 1:28). And in his Ephesian letter he wrote, "I pray that the eyes of your heart may be enlightened" (Eph. 1:18). May this beautiful prayer apply to us as we consider how to use our God-given minds!

Mandates for the Mind

And you shall love the Lord your God with all your heart, and with all your soul, and with all your mind, and with all your strength.
(Mark 12:30)

These words have echoed for thousands of years, beginning with Moses and leading to Jesus. They contain the first of what I call *Mandates for the Mind:* Strive to know God.

To love someone, we must "know" him or her. In the case of my wife, for instance, it would have been absurd to declare that I loved her before I'd ever met her. My love for her implies an intimate knowledge *about* and *of* her. In the same manner, we are to strive both to know *about* God and to "know" Him intimately. Our minds are crucial to this mandate. One of the major problems in contemporary

Christianity is that too many of us are attempting to know God without using our minds to investigate what He has told us of Himself in Scripture.

The second mandate is that the Christian mind should strive for truth. "So Jesus was saying to those Jews who had believed Him, 'If you continue in My word, then you are truly disciples of Mine; and you will know the truth, and the truth will make you free'" (John 8:31–32). Abiding in His word implies a continual dedication to using the mind to search the Scriptures, where His truth resides.

The third mandate pertains to maturity. Romans 12:2 declares: "And do not be conformed to this world, but be transformed by the renewing of your mind, so that you may prove what the will of God is, that which is good and acceptable and perfect" (Rom. 12:2). It is pertinent to note that the words "conformed," "transformed," and "prove" refer to continuous action. Thus, the Christian mind is to be characterized by continuous development toward maturity. In describing the mature mind, the author of Hebrews 5:14 refers to Scripture as "solid food." He then asserts that the Christian is to "press on [continually] to maturity" (Heb. 6:1). Such maturity is a strategic need in the contemporary church.

A fourth mandate involves proclaiming and defending the faith. Maturing Christian minds will actively engage the minds of those around them. For example, Paul modeled this task while in Athens: "So he was reasoning in the synagogue with the Jews and the God-fearing Gentiles, and in the market place every day with those who happened to be present. And also some of the Epicurean and Stoic philosophers were conversing with him" (Acts 17:17–18). Paul proclaimed and defended the truth of the gospel in the synagogue with his own people, among the populace, and even with the intellectual elite of the time. Such encounters are easily duplicated in our day.

The fifth mandate refers to the need for study. Philippians 4:8 states: ". . . whatever is true, whatever is honorable, whatever is right, whatever is pure, whatever is lovely, whatever is of good repute, if there is any excellence and if anything worthy of praise, dwell on these things." Note the final phrase, "dwell on these things," a clause indicative of the need for concentration, or study. The phrase also includes a command that such study is to be continuous. We are to ponder, or think on, the things of God.

Applying the Christian Mind

Prove yourselves doers of the word, and not merely hearers who delude themselves.
(James 1:22)

This exhortation from the book of James includes the sixth and last of our *Mandates for the Mind.* That is, the Christian mind should be applied. Or, what is in the mind should flow to the feet.

It would be easy to state that such a mandate applies to all of life and let that suffice, but specific examples can help us focus on how this mandate works. Therefore, we will focus on three contrived stories.

Our first story involves a fellow we will call Billy. Billy is an excellent softball player. Three nights a week he plays for his company team. He has a reputation as a fierce competitor who will do virtually anything to win. He also has a volatile temper that explodes in ways that embarrass his family and teammates. On some occasions he even has had shoving and cursing bouts with opposing players. Each Sunday, and even on other occasions, he attends a well-known church in his city. One Sunday, his pastor shares an exceptional sermon based on 1 Corinthians 3:16: "Do you not know that you are a temple of God and that the Spirit of God dwells in you?" Upon hearing this message, Billy suddenly realizes that softball games cannot be isolated from his commitment to Christ. Whether in his business, his family, or his softball games, he needs to stop and *think:* If he is a temple of God, all of life is a sacred task. His life, including softball, is never the same.

The second story focuses on a woman named Sally. She is a young elementary public school teacher who also is a young Christian. Her new life in Christ has invigorated her to the point where she is beginning to think of ways she can share her joy with her students. She decides that at every opportunity she will encourage the children to discover the wonder of life. As she guides them through science, she expresses awe as they investigate the simplest flower or the profundity of the solar system. As she discusses arithmetic, she encourages them to realize the beauty of logical order in numbers. As she reads stories to them, she gently emphasizes the amazing concept of human imagination. In these and other ways Sally begins to realize the excitement of using her mind for God's glory. In addition, she soon finds that she is having conversations with her students that give her opportunities to share the One who is guiding her.

Our third story concerns Steven, a businessman and the father of an eight-year-old boy. Steven has come to the realization that his son, Jimmy, spends most of his time either watching television or playing computer games. So he begins to consider ways to stimulate Jimmy's thinking. Since he also wants to see Jimmy come to faith in Christ, Steven suggests that they read C. S. Lewis's Chronicles of Narnia together. Soon the two of them are delighting in these tales, and Steven finds ways to discuss the spiritual metaphors in Lewis's classic fantasies.

These stories might not apply directly to you at this time. But the hope is that they will stimulate a broader understanding of how your mind can be used for God's glory within the routines of life.

6

Human Nature

Don Closson

I n the twenty-five years before 1993, the federal government spent 2.5 trillion dollars on welfare and aid to
cities. This was enough money to buy all of the assets of
the top Fortune 500 firms and all of the farmland in
America at that time.[1] One of the government's goals for
the great War on Poverty, begun by the Johnson administration in the 1960s, was to reduce the number of poor
and the effects of poverty on American society. As one
administration official put it, "The way to eliminate poverty
is to give the poor people enough money so that they won't
be poor anymore."[2]

This goal sounds simple. But offering money didn't
get rid of poverty; in fact, just the opposite has occurred.
The number of children covered by the Aid to Families
with Dependent Children program has gone from 4.5 percent
of all children in America in 1965 to almost 13 percent of
all children in 1991. One of the reasons for this increase
has been the rapid deterioration of the family for those
most affected by the welfare bureaucracy. Since 1960, the
number of single-parent families has more than tripled,
reflecting high rates of children born out of wedlock and
high divorce rates.[3] Rather than strengthening the family

in America and ridding the country of poverty, the War on Poverty produced just the opposite results. Why such disastrous results from such good intentions?

Part of the answer must be found in human nature itself. Might it be that those who created the welfare policy in the 1960s had a faulty view of human nature and thus misread what the solution to poverty should be? In this chapter, I look at how three different worldviews—theism, naturalism, and pantheism—perceive human nature. The worldview we adopt—both individually and nationally —will have a great influence on how we educate our children, how (and if) we punish criminals, and how we run our government.

Christian theism is often chided as being simplistic and lacking in sophistication; yet, on this subject, it is the naturalist and the pantheist who tend to be simplistic. Both will simplify human nature in a way that detracts from our uniqueness and God-given purpose here on this planet. The views of Christian theists, of naturalists, and of pantheists are mutually exclusive. They might all be wrong, but they cannot all be right. The naturalist sees humankind as a biological machine that has evolved by chance. The pantheist perceives humankind as forgetful deity whose essence is a complex series of energy fields that are hidden by an illusion of this apparent physical reality. Christian theism accepts the reality of both our physical and spiritual natures, presenting a balanced, livable view of what it means to be human.

Let's consider how Christian theism, naturalism, and pantheism answer three important questions concerning the nature of humanity. First, are humans special in any way, and do we have a purpose and an origin that sets us apart from the rest of the animal world? Second, are we good, evil, or neither? Third, what happens when we die? These fundamental questions have been asked since the written word appeared and the answers to them are central to what we believe about ourselves.

Are Humans Special?

One doesn't usually think of Hollywood's *Terminator*, as portrayed by Arnold Schwarzenegger, as a profound thinker. Yet in *Terminator II* the robot, sent back from the future to protect a young boy, asks a serious question.

> **Boy:** You were going to kill that guy!
>
> **Terminator:** Of course! I'm a terminator.
>
> **Boy:** Listen to me very carefully, OK? You're not a terminator anymore. All right? You got that?! You just can't go around killing people!
>
> **Terminator:** Why?
>
> **Boy:** What do ya mean, Why? 'Cause you can't!
>
> **Terminator:** Why?
>
> **Boy:** Because you just can't, OK? Trust me on this![4]

Indeed, why not terminate people? Why are they special? To a naturalist, one who believes that no spiritual reality exists, options for answering this question are few. Natural scientists such as astronomer Carl Sagan and entomologist E. O. Wilson find human beings to be no more than products of time plus chance, accidents of mindless evolution. Psychologist Sigmund Freud and existentialist philosopher Jean-Paul Sartre agreed that humankind is a biological machine, perhaps slightly more complex than other animals but governed by the same physical needs and drives.

Yet as Mr. Spock of *Star Trek* fame put it in the original *Star Trek* movie, logic and knowledge aren't always enough. He discovered this by mind-melding with V-GER, a man-made machine that, after leaving our solar system, evolves into a thinking machine elsewhere in the galaxy and returns to earth to find its creator.[5]

If logic and knowledge aren't enough, where do we turn for significance or purpose? A naturalist has nowhere to turn. For example, Sartre argued that human beings must make their own meaning in the face of an absurd universe.[6] The best that entomologist E. O. Wilson could come up with is that we do whatever it takes to pass on our genetic code, our DNA, to the next generation. Everything we do is based on promoting survival and reproduction.[7]

Pantheists have a very different response to the question of human purpose or uniqueness. Dr. Brough Joy, a medical doctor who has accepted an Eastern view of reality, believes that all life-forms are divine, consisting of complex energy fields. In fact, the entire universe is ultimately made up of this energy; the appearance of physical reality is really an illusion.[8] Gerald Jampolsky, another doctor, argues that love is the only part of us that is real, but love itself cannot be defined.[9] This is all very consistent with pantheism, which teaches a radical monism, that all is one, and all is god. But if all is god, all is just as it is supposed to be. Thus Bhagwan Shree Rajneesh can state,

> There is no purpose to life; existence is non-
> purposive. That is why it is called a *leela,* a
> play. Existence itself has no purpose to ful-
> fill. It is not going anywhere—there is no
> end that it is moving toward.[10]

Christianity teaches that human beings are unique. We are created in God's image and for a purpose—to glorify God. Genesis 1:26 declares our image-bearing nature and our mandate to rule over the other creatures of God's creation. Jesus further delineated our purpose when he gave us the two commandments to love God with all of our heart, soul, mind, and strength and to love our neighbor as ourselves. Romans 12:1 calls us to be living sacrifices to God. Unlike naturalism or pantheism, the Bible doesn't reduce us either to our material, physical nature or our spiritual nature. Christianity recognizes the real complexity of humanity as it is found in our physical, emotional, and spiritual components.

Are We Good, Bad, or Neither?

To a naturalist, the notion of good and evil can apply only to the question of survival. If something promotes survival, it is good; if not, it is evil. The only real question is how malleable human behavior is. B. F. Skinner, a Harvard psychology professor, believed that humans are completely programmable via classical conditioning methods. A newborn baby can be conditioned to become a doctor, lawyer, or serial killer, depending on his or her environment.[11]

The movie that won the Best Picture award in 1970 was a response to Skinner's theories. *A Clockwork Orange* depicted a brutal criminal being subjected to a conditioning program that would create a violent physical reaction to the mere thought of doing harm to another person. The following is a conversation between the prison warden and an Anglican clergyman after a demonstration of the therapy's effectiveness.

> **Clergyman:** Choice! The boy has no real choice!
> Has he? Self interest! The fear of
> physical pain drove him to that
> grotesque act of self-abasement!
> Its insincerity was clearly to be seen.
> He ceases to be a wrongdoer.
> He ceases also to be a creature capable
> of moral choice.
>
> **Warden:** Padre, these are subtleties! We're not
> concerned with motives for the higher
> ethics. We are concerned only with
> cutting down crime! (Crowd Applause)
> And with relieving the ghastly congestion
> in our prisons! He will be your true
> Christian. Ready to turn the other
> cheek! Ready to be crucified rather
> than crucify! Sick to the very heart at
> the thought even of killing a fly!
> Reclamation! Joy before the angels of
> God! The point is that it works![12]

Stanley Kubrick denounced this shallow view of human nature with this film, yet Skinner's behaviorism actually allows for more human flexibility than does the sociobiology of E. O. Wilson, another Harvard professor. Wilson asserts that human emotions and ethics, in a general sense, have been programmed to a "substantial degree" by our evolutionary experience.[13] In other words, human beings are hard-coded to respond to conditions by their evolutionary history. Good and evil seem to be beside the point.

Jean-Paul Sartre, another naturalist, rejected the limited view of the sociobiologist, believing that humans, if anything, are choosing-machines. We are completely free to decide who we shall be, whether a drunk in the gutter or a ruler of nations. However, our choice is meaningless. Being a drunk is no better or worse than being a ruler. Since there is no ultimate meaning to the universe, there can be no moral value ascribed to a given set of behaviors.[14]

Pantheists also have a difficult time with this notion of good and evil. Dr. Brugh Joy has written,

> In the totality of Beingness there is no absolute anything—no rights or wrongs, no higher or lower aspects—only the infinite interaction of forces, subtle and gross, that have meaning only in relationship to one another.[15]

The Bhagwan Shree Rajneesh wrote, "I am totally passive. Whatsoever happens, happens. I never question why, because there is no one to be asked."[16]

Christianity teaches that the universe was created by a personal, moral Creator God and that it was created good. This includes humanity. But now creation is in a fallen state due to rebellion against God. This means that humans are inclined to sin and, indeed, are born in a state of sinfulness. It explains mankind's potential goodness and internal sense of justice, as well as our inclination toward evil.

What Happens at Death?

Bertrand Russell wrote more than seventy books on everything from geometry to marriage. Historian Paul Johnson has said that no other intellectual in history offered advice to humanity over so long a period as Bertrand Russell. Holding to naturalist assumptions caused an obvious tension in Russell regarding human nature. He wrote that people are "tiny lumps of impure carbon and water dividing their time between labor to postpone their normal dissolution and frantic struggle to hasten it for others."[17] Yet Russell also wrote the following lines shortly before his death:

> Three passions, simple but overwhelmingly strong, have governed my life: the longing for love, the search for knowledge, and un-bearable pity for the suffering of mankind.[18]

One has to ask why he would pity these self-centered lumps of impure carbon and water.

Most people over forty begin to question the nature and consequence of death. Some people become obsessed with it. A movie called *Flatliners* focused on what death might hold for us. It involved a number of young doctors willing to die temporarily to find out what was on the other side.

Young Doctor #1: Wait a minute! Wait! Quite simply, why are you doing this?

Young Doctor #2: Quite simply to see if there is anything out there beyond death. Philosophy failed! Religion failed! Now it's up to the physical sciences. I think mankind deserves to know![19]

Philosophy has failed, religion has failed, and now its science's turn to find the answers. But what can naturalism offer us? Whether we accept the sociobiology of Wilson or the existentialism of Sartre, death means extinction. If nothing exists beyond the natural, material universe, our death is final and complete.

Pantheists, on the other hand, find death to be a minor inconvenience on the road to *nirvana*. Reincarnation happens to all living things, either moving them toward *nirvana* or further from it, depending on the *karma* accrued in the current life. Although *karma* may include ethical components, it focuses on the realization of oneness with the universe as expressed in actions and thoughts. Depending on the particular view held, attaining *nirvana* is likened to a drop of water being placed in an ocean. All identity is lost; only a radical oneness exists.

Christianity denies the possibility of reincarnation and rejects naturalism's material-only universe. Hebrews 9:27 states, "Man is destined to die once, and after that to face judgment" (NIV). It has always held to a linear view of history, allowing for each person to live a single life, experience death, and then be judged by God. Revelation 20:11–12 records John's vision of the final judgment: "Then I saw a great white throne and him who was seated on it. Earth and sky fled from his presence, and there was no place for them. And I saw the dead, great and small, standing before the throne, and books were opened. Another book was opened, which is the book of life. The dead were judged according to what they had done as recorded in the books" (NIV).

All three versions of what happens at death may be wrong, but they certainly can't all be right! We believe that based on the historical evidence for Christ's life and the dealings of God with the nation of Israel, the biblical account is trustworthy. We believe that those who have placed their faith in the redemptive work of Christ on the cross will spend eternity in glorified bodies worshiping and fellowshipping with their Creator God.

Evaluation and Summary

In his autobiography, entomologist E. O. Wilson writes that as a young man he accepted Christ as his Savior, but because of what he perceived to be hypocrisy in the pulpit he walked away from the church shortly after being baptized. Later, at Harvard University, he sat through a sermon by Dr. Martin Luther King Sr. and then a series of gospel songs sung by students from the campus. He writes that he silently wept while the songs were being sung and said to himself, "These are my people."[20] Wilson claims to be a naturalist, arguing that God doesn't exist; yet he has feelings that he can't explain and desires that do not fit his sociobiological paradigm. Even the staunchly atheistic Jean-Paul Sartre, on his deathbed, had doubts about the existence of God and human significance. Naturalism is a hard worldview to live by.

In 1991, Dr. L. D. Rue addressed the American Association for the Advancement of Science and he advocated that we deceive ourselves with "A Noble Lie"—a lie that deceives us, tricks us, compels us beyond self-interest, beyond ego, beyond family, nation, and race. "It is a lie, because it tells us that the universe is infused with value (which is a great fiction), because it makes a claim to universal truth (when there is none), and because it tells us not to live for self-interest (which is evidently false). 'But without such lies, we cannot live.'"[21] This is the predicament of modern man; either he lives honestly without hope of significance, or he creates a lie that gives a veneer of meaning. As William Lane Craig writes in his book *Reasonable Faith,*

> Man cannot live consistently and happily as though life was ultimately without meaning, value or purpose. If we try to live consistently within the atheistic worldview, we shall find ourselves profoundly unhappy. If instead we manage to live happily, it is only by giving the lie to our worldview.[22]

The pantheist is little better off. Although pantheism claims a spiritual reality, it does so by denying our personhood. We become just another impersonal force field in an unending field of forces. Life is not going anywhere nor is there hope that evil will be judged. Everything just is; let it be.

Neither system can speak out against the injustices of the world because neither sees humankind as significant. Justice implies moral laws and a lawgiver, things that both systems deny exist. One cannot have justice without moral truth. Of the three systems, only Judeo-Christian thought provides the foundation for combating the oppression of other humans.

In J. I. Packer's *Knowing God,* Packer argues that human beings were created to function spiritually as well as physically. Just as we need food, water, exercise, and rest for our bodies to thrive, we need to experience worship, praise, and godly obedience to live spiritually. The result of ignoring these needs will be the dehumanizing of the soul, the development of a brutish rather than a saintly demeanor. Our culture is experiencing this brutishness, this destruction of the soul, on a massive scale. Only revival, which brings about personal devotion to Jesus Christ and the indwelling of the Holy Spirit, will reverse this trend. Because we are truly made in God's image, we will find peace and fulfillment only when we are rightly related to Him.

7

The Breakdown of Religious Knowledge

Todd A. Kappelman

There is a sense among many people today that the modern era, both in terms of technical and financial prosperity, and personal spiritual well-being, is over. There appears to be a general malaise among many people today and a certain uneasy feeling that our culture has entered a new phase. Additionally, most such people believe that this new phase is not a very good one. Many diverse new "communities" such as feminists, gays, pro-choice advocates, pro-life advocates, conservatives, liberals, and various other groups, both religious and nonreligious, make up the global village in which we now live. These various groups are frequently at odds with one another, and more often than not there is a breakdown in communication. This breakdown can be attributed to the lack of a common frame of reference in vocabulary and, more importantly, in views about what constitutes truth.

Most Christians suspect that something is wrong, and although they know that they should continue to engage the culture, they are often at a loss when they try to confront people from different philosophical worldviews because truth itself has come under question. The late Francis Schaeffer wrote a small but extremely important book titled *Escape from Reason* in which he outlined the progression of thought from the late Middle Ages through the 1960s, when the progression culminated in the movement known as existentialism. In this work, Schaeffer noted that the criteria for truth had changed over the years until people found themselves living in an age of *non-reason.* This was an age that had actually become hostile to the very idea of truth and the concept that truths are timeless and not subject to change with the latest fashions of culture.

For much of the nineteenth and twentieth centuries, Darwinian naturalism has been one of the chief philosophical revolutions that gripped the world. And although few people at the time had any idea how much Darwin's ideas would permeate the culture, no one today doubts the far-reaching results of that revolution. The Christian church was not ready for the Darwinian revolution; therefore, this philosophy was able to gain a foothold (and later a death grip) on every aspect of modern life, in both academic and popular circles. For decades after the revolution, many church leaders thought it unimportant to answer Darwin and said little or nothing about the new philosophy. Most Christians were, therefore, not equipped to provide coherent answers and were too late in entering the debate. The result is that most of our public schools and universities, and even our political lives, are dominated by the erroneous assumption that Darwinian naturalism is scientifically true and that creationism is fictitious.

Now, in the late twentieth and early twenty-first century, we are in the middle of a revolution that will likely dwarf Darwinism in its impact on every aspect of thought and culture. The revolution is *postmodernism,* and the danger it holds in its most serious form is that truth, meaning, and objective reality do not exist and that all religious beliefs and moral codes are subjective. The church has had to deal with its particular heresies in every generation, and postmodern relativism is the current heresy. Christ has called us to proclaim truth to a dying generation, and if we fail at this task, relativism and a contempt for reason may overshadow the twenty-first century as much as Darwinian naturalism overshadowed the twentieth century.

From the Premodern Era to the Modern Era

Historians, philosophers, theologians, sociologists, and many others use the terms *premodern, modern,* and *postmodern* to help them navigate through large periods of time and thought. To understand the uses of these very helpful terms, we will try to understand the premodern period first. The term *premodern* is used to describe the period before the Enlightenment of the seventeenth and eighteenth centuries. The premodern period is often referred to as the precritical period—a time before the criteria of truth became so stringent. The premodern period ends somewhere between the invention of the printing press in the fifteenth century and the High Renaissance in the sixteenth century. The major fact that one should remember is that, with the advent of new scientific discoveries, the Western world was changing forever, and these changes would have a far-reaching impact on every aspect of life, especially religion.

Life in the premodern period was dominated by a belief in the supernatural realm, in God or gods, and in His or their activity in human and cosmic affairs. The printing press had not been invented, and the truth or falsity of these gods was largely communicated through oral tradition and hand-written texts that were extremely rare and precious. One can imagine daily or weekly events at which the elders of a tribe or village would gather and share stories with the younger members of the tribe. Typically, these stories contained important matters of faith and history that provided a structure, or worldview, to help the people make sense of their world. These tales also included instructions or moral codes concerning the behavior that was expected for the community to live in peace.

One of the most interesting features about the premodern period is the way in which people decided if the stories that were shared among them were true or false. Imagine that someone had just told you that the world was created by a being that you could not detect with your five senses and that He had left a written communication about His will for your life. You would look around at the world you lived in, and you would decide if the stories that were told to you explained the world and were reasonably believable. This method for determining truth is called the *correspondence method of truth.* If the story being told corresponds to the observable phenomenon in the world, then the story is accepted as truth. There was also a *coherence method of truth* in operation during this period. The coherence theory would add to the correspondence theory the idea that all of the individual stories told over a period of time should not contradict one another. These two forms of determining whether something is true were the primary means of evaluation for many centuries.

We may also look at the premodern period of human history as the *precritical period,* a time before the criteria of truth was based on the scientific method. The premodern period is often characterized as backward and somewhat inferior to modern society. And although the premodern period is not a time period in which most of us would want to live, there is a certain advantage to having the test for truth based on oral and written tradition that corresponds to physical reality. For example, it is easy to see how something such as the creation stories and the gospel would fare much better in the premodern period than in the modern period.

The Advent of the Modern Era

Some people see the modern era as beginning in the Renaissance of the fifteenth and sixteenth centuries. Others, however, believe it began with the Enlightenment of the seventeenth and eighteenth centuries.

A main tenet of *modernism* is that human reason, armed with the scientific method, is the only reliable means of attaining knowledge about the universe. During the Renaissance, men began to discover the means to harness the powers and resources of the earth in ever increasing ways. It was a time marked by invention and discovery that led to what may be termed an optimistic humanism, or a high confidence in mankind. The Enlightenment followed the Renaissance, when better telescopes and microscopes allowed men to unlock the secrets of the universe. The unlocking of these secrets led to the initial impression that both the universe and the human body resembled machines and could be understood in mechanistic terms.

In the eighteenth century, the progress of science accelerated so rapidly that it appeared as if science would soon be able to explain everything. Many people believed that there were no limits to the power of human reason operating with the data from sense perception. In contrast to the truth of the oral tradition in the premodern era, the modern period accepted as truth only that which could be proven to be true with the senses. Many of the philosophers and theologians of the modern period sought to devise a rational religion, a faith that could incorporate all of the considerations and discoveries of the new science.

The effort of the Enlightenment rationalists to synthesize the new scientific method with the premodern religious beliefs soon resulted in a suspicion of the claims of the Christian religion to oral and written truth. It is easy to see how doctrines such as the virgin birth, the deity of Christ, and the resurrection could not be proved using scientific methods. There is no way to repeat such historical events in a laboratory environment; therefore, the credibility of such events became suspect.

The modern industrial revolution yielded new labor-saving inventions regularly. These new discoveries substantiated the optimism of the modernists and gave credence to the belief that science and the scientific method would one day yield a utopian society. It is easy to see how the optimism of this period became almost intoxicating to many people. The so-called "truths" of religion were quickly being cast aside in favor of the new and better "truths" found by science. Examples found in advertising may be helpful in understanding this change. A company that wanted to sell a car or a pair of tennis shoes would appeal to the scientific truths of their product. It would attempt to persuade a potential buyer into purchasing its product based on the fact that it was the best item obtainable. Add to this scientific furor the advancement of Darwinian naturalism, and it is easy to see how religious claims seemed like quaint, antiquated beliefs for many people.

The modern period culminated in arrogance concerning human abilities and human reason. It proposed a world created without any assistance from God. The modern period differs from the premodern in its rejection of the supernatural or the transcendent, based largely on the belief that claims of religious truth are different from claims of scientific truth. According to many people, truth itself had changed.

The End of the Modern Era and the Advent of the Postmodern Era

Many factors contributed to the end of the modern period and the demise of the Enlightenment confidence that had driven Western development for more than three centuries. The major force behind the advance of modernism was the belief that reality was objective and that all men could discover the principles of nature and unlock her secrets.

According to many postmodernists, the failure of the modern ideal was due to the erroneous assumption that there is such a thing as "objective truth." Following the Romantic and Existentialist movements, the postmodernists built their theories of reality on the latest discoveries in language, culture, psychotherapy, and even cutting-edge science. Theories in quantum physics, radically different views about cultural norms, and ethnic differences contributed to the belief that claims of truth are much more relative than the Enlightenment thinkers had believed. Many people believed that science had substantiated relativity.

Modernity may be understood as a time when our best philosophers, theologians, and scientists attempted to make sense of the world based on the belief in objective reality. One of the central tenets of the era in which we live (the postmodern period) is that there is no such thing as objective truth. In fact, the new trend in postmodern thought is to embrace, affirm, and live with philosophical, theological, and even scientific chaos. Earlier we used an example from advertising, suggesting that products were marketed based on their claims of superiority over what a competitor might offer. If we use this example again, postmodern methodology appeals more to a person's feelings than to his or her sense of factual truth. Cars, tennis shoes, and other products are marketed based on image. The best car is not necessarily the one that has been made to the highest standard; rather, the best car is the one that can bolster the image of the driver.

The effects of this type of thinking may be seen in our contemporary ethical dilemma. While it is true that people from various ethnic groups, geographic areas, and other time periods place different values on certain behaviors, it cannot be true that any behavior is acceptable, dependent only upon the individual's outlook. The effect of postmodern theories on claims of Christian truth is that the creation accounts found in Genesis and the stories about Christ in the Gospels have been reduced to one cultural group's account of reality. Christians, argue many postmodernists, are free to believe that Christ is God if they like. But their claims cannot exclude other people's beliefs. "Truth" may be true for one person and false for another.

Furthermore, Christians are expected to tolerate contradicting claims of truth and to look the other way if certain behaviors (e.g., abortion and homosexuality) do not suit their tastes. The current postmodern condition is only in the early stages of development, not even half a century old, yet its devastating effects have penetrated every aspect of our lives. Christians largely responded too late to the threats of Darwinism, and now the destructive effects of that movement are evident to anyone in the

Christian community. Postmodernism, and its companion, relativism, should be among the foremost concerns of any Christian who wants to engage his or her culture and ensure that the gospel of Christ has a fertile context in which it can take root and grow in the future.

Responding to the Current Crises in Knowledge

A conversation I had with a young woman at Bucknell University provided a perfect example of how our contemporaries differ from their predecessors. This young woman believed that truth was a matter of how one looked at things. She, like so many others, believed that two people could look at a given situation or object and arrive at different conclusions. Although this is true to some degree, it is not true to the extent that the two different claims of truth can logically be contradictions of one another.

When she was pressed on her beliefs concerning reality, the inconsistencies of her philosophy were evident. She stated that everything was a matter of opinion or one's personal perspective. When asked if this belief extended to physical reality, she said it did. She said that a person could look at something in such a way as to alter reality.

The example of the existence or nonexistence of her car was raised. She said that if she believed that her car was not in the parking lot and if another person believed that it was, it was possible that it actually existed for one person and not for the other. When we first hear such reasoning, we might be tempted to think that the person who maintains this position is joking and could not possibly mean for us to take it seriously. However, the sad and frightening truth is that this individual was very serious.

This young woman is representative of a large part of

our Western culture. She is one of many men and women who tend to think unsystematically. The result of this way of thinking is that people often hold ideas that are logically inconsistent and contradictory. Because of this, people who profess to be Buddhists, Christians, Hindus, Jews, or even atheists are given equal credence. Truth has become a function of personal preference, without needing to correspond to objective reality.

The effects of this new way of thinking are evident everywhere. When we attempt to speak to people on any controversial issue—whether it is political, ethical, or religious—we invariably are confronted with different approaches to truth. Some people accept divine revelation, others accept science, and still others accept no final authority. We have moved from fact-based criteria to feelings-based criteria for truth. The final appeal in many disagreements is often a statement such as, "That may be true for you, but it is not true for me." This is an implicit denial of a common ground of reality.

Psalm 11:3 asks what the righteous can do if the foundations have been destroyed. Although the threat of postmodern relativism may be something new, it is not the first time that Christians have seen a concentrated effort to destroy the foundations of truth. The New Testament is replete with admonitions for Christians to allow their behavior to speak for them. John 13:35 says that people will know that we belong to Christ and that our testimony is true by the way we love one another.

The premodern, modern, and postmodern tests for truth all have strengths and weaknesses. But the Scriptures seem to indicate that it is our behavior toward one another and our devotion to God, not our ability to prove God's existence or His actions, that will convince a skeptical postmodern world that hungers for truth.

8

The New Absolutes

Rick Wade

When Christians take a stand on a given moral issue—for instance, on abortion—what are some typical responses? Someone might say, "What right do you have to push *your* morality on the rest of us?" Or another person might say, "Abortion might be wrong for you, but it's not for me."

What these people are implying is that such beliefs are *relative;* that is, they are related to something else—my own desires or circumstances, for example. Because these beliefs change through time, something that is true or good for me today might not be true or good tomorrow. Nothing is true or good for all people at all times.

Have you noticed, however, that many of the same people who claim that truth and morality are relative can be found denouncing certain political views, or actively pushing the social acceptance of a formerly rejected lifestyle, or fighting for new rights in one area or another?

Author William Watkins *has* noticed, and he's recorded his thoughts in a new book titled *The New Absolutes.*[1] Watkins believes that despite the rhetoric, Americans are in fact *not* relativists; we are in reality *absolutists.* He says that, rather than *abandoning* absolutes, we are simply adopting new ones to replace the old.

It is now believed, Watkins says, "that truth and error, right and wrong, beautiful and ugly, normal and abnormal, and a host of other judgments are determined by the individual, her circumstances, or her culture. . . . There is no transcendent God or universal natural law we can point to that can inform us about who we are, what our world is like, and how we should get along in it."[2]

What is the source of this thinking? Watkins points to three elements: a loss of belief in absolute truth, a strong belief in tolerance, and a detachment from people and institutions resulting from pessimism and distrust.

If Americans have concluded that ideas and morals are relative, however, why does Watkins say that Americans are really absolutists? We are betrayed, he says, by our behavior.[3]

A glut of lawsuits in the courts, calls for law and order in politics, moral outrage over various offenses, cries for human rights, and the spreading of liberal democratic ideas to other countries are evidence that Watkins is right. Americans have an idea of what is right, and we think that others should agree with us. Such thinking is not relativism.

More significant, however, is how we can see an absolutist mentality in those who typically espouse relativism. For example, those who scream the loudest for *tolerance* often restrict others to saying and doing only what is politically correct. In the name of *pluralism,* secularists push religion out of the public square. And *multi-culturalists* condemn the West for its cultural practices. It seems that what is sauce for the goose is *not* sauce for the gander.

The average American who has come to accept relativistic notions of truth and morality might fairly be accused of being only inconsistent. But those who are real activists in the current fight for cultural change must bear the charge of blatant hypocrisy.

Old Absolutes Versus New Absolutes

Watkins contrasts ten traditional beliefs (old absolutes) with the ten beliefs that are replacing them. Although these new beliefs might not be "absolutes" in a strict, philosophical sense, they *function* as absolutes in contemporary society.

In this chapter I will look at three of the issues that Watkins discusses—pro-life versus pro-death beliefs, religion in the public square, and political correctness and tolerance —to see if, indeed, proponents are really the relativists they claim to be. As we consider these issues, I think you'll agree with Watkins that the culture war is not being fought between absolutists and relativists but between two groups of absolutists.

Death: What a Beautiful Choice

First, let's consider the pro-life versus pro-death question.

According to Watkins, the old absolute was, "Human life from conception to natural death is sacred and worthy of protection." The new absolute is, "Human life, which begins and ends when certain individuals or groups decide it does, is valuable as long as it is wanted."[4]

Two issues that bring this new belief to the fore are abortion and physician-assisted suicide.[5] Few practices are as fiercely opposed or defended as abortion. Opponents say that abortion is morally wrong for all people. Proponents say that it is a matter of individual choice. Physician-assisted suicide draws similar responses.

It is easy to overstate the thinking of those who espouse the new absolute. Probably very few of them would say that they "love death" or would think of death as a "good" thing, ranking up there, say, with riches and great health and freedom. Rather, death is more often thought of simply as the lesser of two evils.

Nevertheless, many people think of death as a positive thing, as something to be embraced, as the best answer to suffering or to certain hardships that many people experience.

Regardless of whether they think of it as a good thing, however, they think of it as a right not to be tampered with. It is rooted, some say, in a constitutional "right to privacy."

In claiming this right, however, any foundation in relativistic thinking must be abandoned. For the very "right" that proponents claim is itself an absolute. They are saying that the right of individuals to decide for themselves should be observed by everyone else. When they say it is wrong for pro-lifers to try to press their beliefs on others, they are stating an absolute. If they say that the value of human life is a matter of its quality rather than of intrinsic worth, they are stating another absolute.

Some relativists will try to wriggle out of the charge of absolutism by saying that their position might be right for now but not necessarily for all times and all places. Nonetheless, their ideas about the value of human life and the option of death as a solution to human suffering function as absolutes in our society today.

Watkins is correct. The stubbornness with which proponents of abortion and assisted suicide defend their "rights" is good evidence for the claim that Americans, despite all the talk, are not relativists after all.

Freedom from Religion

It used to be held that "religion is the backbone of American culture, providing the moral and spiritual light needed for public and private life." Now, according to Watkins, we have a new absolute: "Religion is the bane of public life, so for the public good it should be banned from the public square."[6]

Certainly there are those who are this adamant about the place of religion. These are the ones who raise a fuss when a prayer is uttered at a public school graduation ceremony, or who complain when a nativity scene is set up on public property at Christmas.

The majority of Americans probably are not this combative about the issue. However, they believe, for a variety of reasons, that religion should be kept separate from public life.

One reason is a misunderstanding of the First Amendment.[7] We have been told over and over again that the separation of church and state requires that the government must not be involved with religious matters in any way. The new absolute is that religion and public policy should be kept separate.

We should notice, however, that strict "separationists" do not talk much about our nation's beginnings. A study of our founding documents shows that religion was an integral part of Americans' lives; references to the Bible and Christian beliefs are often cited in the construction of our new government. Amazingly enough, the writers of the Constitution did not see in that document the wall of separation that current interpreters see.[8]

Another reason why some people think that religion should be kept a private matter is a misunderstanding about religion itself. Having been "schooled" in relativistic thinking, many (perhaps most) Americans believe that whatever they believe is true for them but not necessarily for other people.

But this cannot be so. Religions provide an explanation of what is ultimately *real.* Either there is one true God or there is not. Either there is salvation through Jesus, or there is enlightenment through meditation, or there is some other way to find fulfillment. Not all of these religious views can be true *in reality.*

This issue really gets tangled when we consider the matter of rights. The idea that everyone has the right to worship as he or she chooses has been transformed into meaning that each person's choice of religion is true. "I have the right to believe as I wish" becomes "My belief is as true as yours." The fact that I believe something makes it true.

But is that how things work in other areas of life? If I believe that I am a millionaire, does that make me one? With respect to religion, does my believing that there is a God put Him there? Or does my believing that there is no God produce a godless universe?

The new absolutism with respect to religion is a very real concern for many Americans. As Christians we are taught that our beliefs have meaning for all of life, not just for the prayer closet. Bringing these beliefs out into the public arena has caused some Christians great difficulty.

Ironically, in a nation that began with a strong desire for the free expression of religious beliefs, people are now more and more pressured to leave their beliefs at home.

Does this sound like relativism to you?

The Politically Correct Life

The hypocrisy of the new absolutism is seen more clearly than anywhere else in what is now called "political correctness," or PC.

To be politically correct is to be in line with certain ideals promoted by the new cultural reformers, ideals such as abortion rights, multi-culturalism, feminism, and homosexual rights. To say or do anything that goes against these ideals is to be politically incorrect.[9]

It is easier to understand PC if we think of it as the end of a chain of thinking. First is the acceptance of relativism, the idea that there are no absolutes. This belief, taken with our democratic idea of equality, results in the belief that everyone's beliefs and choices are equal or equally valid. There should be no discrimination against other beliefs or lifestyles. This is the *new tolerance,* the prime virtue of the new reformers.

When history is viewed from this perspective, it seems clear that history is the story of the strong taking advantage of the weak. The weak—or disadvantaged—are victims who now require extra help to attain their rightful place of equality. Merely belonging to a victimized group is enough to expect this extra help regardless of whether a given individual has been victimized. The advantaged must now be sensitive to the "needs" of the disadvantaged to avoid making them feel any more victimized, and they must work to protect their rights. Finally, the advantaged must not do or say anything that could be interpreted as differentiating the disadvantaged, of portraying them as negatively different. To be sensitive to the plight of the oppressed and to avoid doing or saying anything that might make them feel marginalized or inadequate or looked down upon—this is political correctness.

It is certainly true that there have been and are people who oppress others. Such activity must not be allowed. The problem with political correctness, however, lies in over-correcting the problem.

For example, in *The New Absolutes,* Watkins lists some words real estate agents are supposed to avoid in order not to offend potential buyers. For example, *executive* has racist overtones because most executives are white. *Sports enthusiast* might make the disabled feel left out. *Master bedroom* creates images of slavery. *Walk-in closet* could offend people who can't walk.[10]

Author Stan Gaede, in his book *When Tolerance Is No Virtue,* says that "the overt goal of PC . . . is to enforce a uniform standard of tolerance, regardless of race, gender, cultural background or sexual orientation. The problem is that the items on this list . . . are not precisely parallel to each other. Though each is the basis for discrimination in our society, they involve very different kinds of issues. So the question immediately becomes: What does it mean to be tolerant *in each case?* . . . PC allows each group to define tolerance for itself."[11]

We have now come full circle. The relativism that purportedly undergirds the new tolerance gives way to exactly what it was trying to eliminate, namely, absolutes. That is, the reformers make their own ideals the new guidelines for society. We are all expected to abide by them. These are the new absolutes.

How should Christians respond to all of this? Next, we'll look at how the new absolutes are promoted, and we'll think about how we might respond.

Absolutely for the Common Good

It's a myth that America is a relativistic society. The truth is that Americans are a very moralistic people. What is alarming, however, is how cultural reformers are seeking to establish new absolutes that go against traditional absolutes. Watkins shows how these reformers are setting up new rules that we all must follow.

How shall we understand the contradiction between claims of relativism on the one hand and the imposition of new absolutes on the other? Watkins believes that the claim to relativism is an attempt "to rationalize . . . misbehavior and disarm . . . critics."[12] For example, individuals might fall back on relativism to justify sexual activity once held to be deviant. However, the supposed relativist quickly becomes an absolutist when he wants *others* to agree with *him* on a given idea or issue.

But if everything is relative, how are relativists able to convince others of the rightness of their own beliefs? They can't appeal to a foundation of unchanging realities and objective truths and be consistent with their relativism.

So how do they do it? Calling opponents names—"fundamentalist" is a favorite—or repeating simplistic clichés—"safe, legal abortion," for example—are a couple of their favorite means. The media play a strong role in this process, especially television. Captivating images, clever writing, strategically placed laugh tracks, and other elements persuasively convey ideas without logical reasoning.

It is crucial that we step back to see the situation for which these tactics prepare us. If we become conditioned to be persuaded by sloganeering rather than by rational discourse, we are set up to be taken in by any smooth talker. All of our clamoring for rights and for the authority of the individual has the unexpected result of preparing us to *lose* our freedoms at the hands of charismatic tyrants.

What can we do to change things?

First, as Watkins notes, reality itself is on our side.[13] The new absolutes go against the way the universe is. Many women who opt for childlessness, for example, find themselves late in life confronting their own maternal instincts. We can point out such facts to those who believe that we can do anything we want and get along quite nicely.

Second, we can learn to recognize sloganeering and insist that the cultural reformers use sound reason when promoting their ideals.

Third, we can point to the hypocrisy of so-called relativists. Homosexuals who barge into church services, demanding tolerance for their lifestyle, must see how intolerant *they* are. Those who demand freedom of thought and expression for themselves cannot reasonably exclude religious beliefs from public discourse.

As strange as it might sound at first, William Watkins calls us to a renewed *in*tolerance. He says, "We must violate the new tolerance and become people marked by intolerance. Not an intolerance that unleashes hate upon people, but an intolerance that's unwilling to allow error to masquerade as truth. An intolerance that calls evil *evil* and good *good*."[14]

To reestablish the old absolutes, Watkins calls for the acknowledgment of certain beliefs, such as that all life is precious, that relativism is false, that the moral law is real, and that religion is essential. A return to these basics will return us to making sound public policy, to greater civil order, and to moral progress.

Part 2
Leisure

9

Art and the Christian

Jerry Solomon and Jimmy Williams

Where are you as you read this? You may be sitting in an office, reclining in a lounge chair at home, relaxing in your backyard, sitting at a desk in your dorm room, or any other of a number of places. Consider for a moment if art is part of your consciousness. If you are sitting in an office, is art anywhere within your vision? If you are reclining in a lounge chair, does the furniture have an artistic dimension? If you are relaxing in your backyard, can the word *art* be used to describe any facet of what you see? If you are in your dorm room, are you listening to music that is art?

If I had the pleasure of talking with you about these questions, no doubt we would have a very interesting conversation. Some of you might say, "No, art doesn't describe anything I see at the moment." Or, some of you might state, "I haven't thought of this before. You'll have to give me more time for reflection." Others might assert, "I think of art only within museums, concert halls, or other such places that enshrine our art." Others might say, "Yes, art is very much a part of my daily life." But since I can't talk with you to know what you are doing at the moment, and I certainly cannot see what you see, let me tell you where I am and what I see as I write these comments.

I am sitting at my desk in my study while listening to the music of Bach. I see a clock on one of the bookshelves, a hand-painted plate I purchased in the country of Slovenia; a framed poem given to me by my daughter; several chairs; two floor lamps; a mirror with a bamboo frame; two canoe paddles I bought in the San Blas islands off the coast of Panama; a wooden statue I purchased in Ecuador; and a unique, colorful sculpture that my son made. As I mention these things, perhaps you are attempting to imagine them. You are trying to "see" or "hear" them, and in so doing there are certain of these items you may describe as art. Your first response may be to say that the music of Bach, the hand-painted Slovenian plate, or the Ecuadorian statue can be described as art. But what about the chair in which I am sitting, the desk, the bookshelves, the chairs, or the lamps? Better yet, what about items like these that are found where you live? Are they art?

Such questions are indicative of the challenges we face when we begin to consider the place of art in our lives. As an evangelical Christian, I can state that art and the aesthetic dimensions of life have not received much attention within my formal training. Only through my own pursuit have I begun to think about art with a Christian worldview. And I have found that my experience is similar to what many other people have experienced within the evangelical community. Too often we have tended to label art as inconsequential or even detrimental to the Christian life.

Actually, there is nothing new about this tendency. Our spiritual forefathers debated such issues. They were surrounded by Greek and pagan cultures that challenged them to give serious thought to how they should express their new beliefs. Art surrounded them, but could the truth of Christ be expressed legitimately through art? Could

Christians give positive attention to the art of non-Christians? In light of such struggles, my intention is to encourage you to attend to some of the basic elements of a Christian worldview of art and aesthetics in this essay. I believe that you will find our discussion can have significant application in your life.

Art and Aesthetics

Several years ago, I was having dinner with a group of young people when our conversation turned to the subject of music. During the discussion, I commented on how I believe that a qualitative difference exists between the music of Bach and that of a musician who was popular among Christians at the time of our discussion. When one of the students at our table heard this, he immediately responded in anger and accused me of flagrant prejudice and a judgmental spirit. Even though I attempted to elaborate my point, the young man had determined that I was an elitist and would no longer listen.

This incident is a reminder that one of the most prevalent ways of approaching art is simply to say that "beauty is in the eye (or ear) of the beholder." The incident also shows that "good" and "bad," or "beautiful" and "ugly," among other adjectives, are part of our vocabulary when we talk of art. This vocabulary pertains to a field of philosophy called aesthetics.

All of us deal with aesthetics at various times in our lives, and many of us incorporate aesthetic statements in our daily conversations. For example, we may say, "That was a great movie," or, "That was a terrible movie." When we make such statements, we normally don't think seriously about how such terms actually apply to what we have seen. We are stating our opinions, but those opinions are usually the result of an immediate emotional response. The challenge comes when we attempt to relate qualitative statements about the movie as part of a quest to find universal guidelines that can be applied to all art. When we accept this challenge, we begin to explain why some art is great, some merely good, and some not worthwhile at all.

Aesthetics and Nature

Perhaps one of the clearest ways to begin to understand the aesthetic dimension of our lives is to consider how we respond to nature. Have you ever heard anyone say, "That's an ugly sunset"? Probably not, but surely you have heard the word *beautiful* applied to sunsets. And when you hear the phrase *beautiful sunset,* you probably don't hear an argument to the contrary. Usually there is a consensus among those who see a sunset: it is beautiful. From a Christian perspective, those who are there are offering a judgment concerning both the artist and the art. Both the cause and the effect have been praised aesthetically. Torrential waterfalls, majestic mountains, and colorful sunsets routinely evoke a human aesthetic response.

The Christian knows that the very fabric of the universe expresses God's presence with majestic beauty and grandeur. Psalm 19:1 states, "The heavens declare the glory of God; and the firmament shows His handiwork" (NKJV). Nature has been called the "aesthetics of the infinite." Through telescope or microscope, one can devote a lifetime to the study of some part of the universe—the skin, the eye, the sea, the flora and fauna, the stars, the climate. All of nature can be appreciated for its aesthetic qualities that find their source in God, their Creator. In fact, we can assert that "the major premise of a Christian worldview, including a Christian aesthetic, is that God is the Creator."[1]

Human Creativity

"You have a wonderful imagination! Are you an artist?"

Has anyone said such a thing to you? If so, perhaps you responded by saying something that would contradict the person's perception of you. Most of us don't see ourselves as artistic, imaginative people. Indeed, most of us tend to think of *artist* and *imagination* as terms that apply only to certain elite individuals who have left a legacy of work. "The truth is that in discussing the arts we are discussing something universal to mankind."[2] For example, anthropologists tell us that all primitive peoples thought art was important.[3] Why is this true?

From the perspective of a Christian worldview, the answer is found in how we are created. Because we are made in God's image that must include the glorious concept that we, too, are creative. After creating man, God told him to subdue the earth and rule over it. Adam was to cultivate and keep the garden (Gen. 2:15), which God described as "very good" (Gen. 1:31). The implication of this is very important. God, the Creator, a lover of the beauty in His created world, invited Adam, one of His creatures, to share in the process of "creation" with Him. He has permitted humans to take the elements of His cosmos and create new arrangements with them. Perhaps this explains why creating anything is so fulfilling to us. We can express a drive within us, which allows us to do something that all humans uniquely share with their Creator.

God has thus placed before the human race a banquet table rich with aesthetic delicacies. He has supplied the basic ingredients, inviting those made in His image to exercise their creative capacities to the fullest possible extent. We are privileged as no other creature to make and enjoy art.

There is a dark side to this, however, because sin

entered and affected all of human life. A bent and twisted nature has emerged, tainting every field of human endeavor or expression and consistently marring the results. The unfortunate truth is that divinely endowed creativity will always be accompanied in earthly life by the reality and presence of sin expressed through a fallen race. Man is Jekyll and Hyde: a noble image-bearer and a morally crippled creature. Therefore, his works of art are bittersweet.

Understanding this dichotomy allows Christians genuinely to appreciate something of the contribution of every artist, composer, or author. God is sovereign and dispenses unique artistic talents upon whom He will. While Scripture keeps us from emulating certain lifestyles of artists or condoning some of their ideological perspectives, we can nevertheless admire and appreciate their talent, which ultimately finds its source in God.

The fact is that if God can speak through a burning bush or Balaam's donkey, He can speak through a hedonistic artist! The question can never be how worthy the vessel is but rather whether truth has been expressed. God's truth is still sounding forth today from the Bible, from nature, and even from fallen humanity.

Because of the Fall, absolute beauty in the world is gone. But participation in the aesthetic dimension reminds us of the beauty that once was and anticipates its future luster. Surrounded by beauty that can take one's breath away, even in this unredeemed world, one can but speculate about what lies ahead for those who love Him!

Art and the Bible

What does the Bible have to say about the arts? Happily, the Bible does not call upon Christians to look down upon the arts. In fact, the arts are imperative when considered from the biblical mandate that whatever we do should be done to the glory of God (1 Cor. 10:31). We are to offer Him the best that we have—intellectually, artistically, and spiritually. Furthermore, at the very center of Christianity stands the Incarnation ("the Word made flesh"), an event that identified God with the physical world and gave dignity to it. A real Man died on a real cross and was laid in a real, rock-hard tomb. The Greek ideas of "other-worldlyness" that fostered a tainted and debased view of nature (hence, aesthetics) find no place in biblical Christianity. Therefore, the dichotomy between sacred and secular is alien to biblical faith. Paul's statement "Unto the pure, all things are pure" (Titus 1:15 KJV) includes the arts. Although we may recognize that human creativity, like all other gifts bestowed upon us by God, may be misused, there is nothing inherently or more sinful about the arts than any other areas of human activity.

The Old Testament

The Old Testament is rich with examples that confirm the artistic dimension. Exodus 25 shows that God commanded beautiful architecture along with other forms of art (metalwork, clothing design, tapestry, and so on) in the building of the tabernacle and eventually the temple. Here we find something unique in history: art works conceived and designed by the infinite God, then transmitted to and executed by His human apprentices!

Poetry is another evidence of God's love for beauty. A large portion of the Old Testament—including Psalms, Proverbs, Ecclesiastes, Song of Solomon, portions of the prophets, and Job contain poetry. Because God inspired the very words of Scripture, it logically follows that He inspired the poetical form in such passages.

Music and dance also are found in the Old Testament.

In Exodus 15, the children of Israel celebrated God's Red Sea victory over the Egyptians with singing, dancing, and playing of instruments. In 1 Chronicles 23:5, we find musicians in the temple, their instruments specifically made by King David for praising God. And we should remember that the lyrical poetry of the Psalms was first intended to be sung.

The New Testament

The New Testament also includes artistic insights. The most obvious is the example of Jesus Himself. First, He was by trade a carpenter, a skilled craftsman (Mark 6:3). Second, His teachings were full of examples that reveal His sensitivity to the beauty all around: the fox, the bird nest, the lily, the sparrow and the dove, the glowering skies, a vine, and a mustard seed. Jesus was also a master story-teller. He readily made use of His own cultural setting to impart His message, sometimes quite dramatically. Many of the parables were fictional stories; nevertheless, they were used to teach spiritual truths via the imagination.

We should also remember that the entire Bible is not only revelation but also itself a work of art. And this work of art "has been the single greatest influence on art. It sheds more light upon the creative process and the use of the arts than any other source, because in it are found the great truths about man as well as God that are the well-springs of art."[4]

Evaluating Art

Can the Bible help us evaluate art? Consider the concepts found in Philippians 4:8:

> Finally, brethren, whatever is true, whatever
> is honorable, whatever is right, whatever is

> pure, whatever is lovely, whatever is of good
> repute, if there is any excellence and if any-
> thing worthy of praise, let your mind dwell
> on these things.

Let's concentrate for a few moments on this verse to see if it might at least provide the beginning of a framework for the evaluation and enjoyment of art.

Paul begins with truth. When considering art, the Christian is compelled to ask, "Is this really true?" Does life genuinely operate in this fashion in light of God's revelation? And Christians must remember that truth includes the negatives as well as the positives of reality.

Paul then moves on to the concept of honor or dignity. This can refer to what we related earlier in this essay about the nature of humankind: we have dignity even though we are sinful. This gives a basis, for example, for rejecting the statements in the work of the artist Francis Bacon. Bacon painted half-truths. He presented deterioration and hopeless despair, but he didn't present man's honor and dignity.

The third key to aesthetic comprehension has to do with the moral dimension—what is right. Not all art makes a moral statement, but when it does Christians must deal with it, not ignore it. For example, Picasso's painting *Guernica* is a powerful moral statement protesting the bombing by the Germans of a town by that name just prior to World War II. Protesting injustice is a cry for justice.

Purity is the fourth concept. It also touches on the moral—by contrasting that which is innocent, chaste, and pure with that which is sordid, impure, and worldly. For instance, one need not be a professional drama critic to identify and appreciate the fresh, innocent love of Romeo and Juliet or to distinguish it from the erotic escapades of a Tom Jones.

Whereas the first four concepts have dealt with facets of artistic statements, the fifth concept focuses on sheer beauty: "Whatever is lovely." If there is little to evaluate morally and rationally, we are still free to appreciate what is beautiful in art.

The sixth concept, that of good repute, gives us impetus to evaluate the life and character of the artist. The less-than-exemplary lifestyle of an artist may somewhat tarnish his artistic contribution, but it doesn't necessarily obliterate it. The greatest art is true, skillfully expressed, imaginative, and unencumbered by the personal and emotional problems of its originators.

Excellence is yet another concept. It is a comparative term; it assumes that something else is not excellent. The focus is on quality, which is worth much discussion. But one sure sign of it is craftsmanship—technical mastery. Another sign is durability; great art lasts.

The last concept is praise. Here we are concerned with the impact or the effect of the art. Great art can have power and is therefore a forceful tool of communication. Herein lies the "two-edged sword" of art. It can inspire a culture, or it can help bring a culture to ruin. Paul undergirds this meaty verse by stating that we should let our minds "dwell on these things," a reminder that Christianity thrives on intelligence, not ignorance, even in the artistic realm.

Thus, our hope is that we will pursue the artistic dimensions of our lives with intelligence and imagination. The world needs to see and hear from Christians who are committed to art for the glory of God.

10

Music and the Christian

Jerry Solomon

Music is a pervasive part of contemporary culture. We hear it on elevators, in restaurants, in offices, in hotel lobbies, on telephones while we wait for our party to answer, and in virtually every other corner of contemporary life. In fact, it permeates the airwaves so thoroughly that we often do not realize it is there.

Television uses music not only in musical programs but also in commercials and program soundtracks. Movies use music to enhance the events shown on the screen. Radio offers a wide variety of music around the clock. The availability of recordings allows us to program music to suit our own listening tastes, and we can hear them in virtually any location. Concerts, especially in large cities, offer a potpourri of music from which to choose.

There are also many musical genres. Rock (with its assortment of styles and labels), rap, country and western, jazz, Broadway, folk, classical, New Age, and gospel provide us with a dizzying assortment of listening and performing options. Such permeation and variety provide us with a unique opportunity to practice discernment. Some people might think that discernment is unnecessary because they claim to listen only to "Christian" music. Nevertheless, the broader population of the evangelical community spends innumerable hours absorbing music, whether "Christian" or "secular."

Why should a Christian be interested and involved in the arts, and in music in particular? In his excellent work *Theology and Contemporary Art Forms,* John Newport lists several helpful points:

> The first reason Christians should be interested in the arts is related to the biblical teaching that God reveals and carries on his redemptive purpose in time and history. The Christian community . . . cannot cut itself off from the characteristic artistic vitalities of history—past and present. Second . . . the arts give a peculiarly direct access to the distinctive tone, concerns, and feelings of a culture. . . . The artists not only mirror their age in its subtlest nuances, but they generally do it a generation ahead of more abstract and theoretical thinkers. Third . . . the arts focus (in a remarkably vivid and startling way) on the vital issues and themes which are the central concern of theology. Fourth . . . the arts spell out dramatically the implications of various worldviews.[1]

The second, third, and fourth points are especially applicable to music. If music mirrors culture, if it tells us of important issues and themes, and if it shows the implications of various worldviews, it can tell us a great deal about our culture. Lyrically, music can be used as a medium for criticism, commendation, reflection, questioning, rebellion, and any number of other thoughts or emotions. When musical language is employed to relay these thoughts or emotions the result can be significant.

History is replete with examples of the ways music has been vitally employed in various cultures. One of the more prominent examples of this can be found in the Psalms, where lyrics were merged with music to form a strategic voice for Israel's life. The same is true in contemporary life. The themes of rock, rap, and country music demonstrate how music can be a notable voice for the spirit of a culture, whether for good or evil.

To affect our culture, we must listen to that voice. We must hear its questions and be sensitive to the needs that cry out for the answers God provides.

Can Music Be "Christian"?

One of the continuing debates among evangelicals centers on how music is to be judged. Some people say that there is a particular musical style that is distinctly Christian; others reject such a proposition. Some people believe that certain musical styles are intrinsically evil; others reject this idea. The examples of this conflict are numerous. It is important that we join the dialogue. In the process, we will observe several ways we should respond to the music of our culture.

First, the term "Christian music" is a misnomer. Music cannot be declared Christian because of particular ingredients. There is no Christian melody, harmony, rhythm, or any other aspect of musical syntax. There is no distinctive sound that makes a piece of music Christian. The only part of a composition that can make it Christian is the lyrics. In view of the fact that such phrases as "contemporary Christian music" are in vogue, this is a meaningful observation. Perhaps the phrase "contemporary Christian lyrics" would be more appropriate. Of course, the lyrics could be poor doctrinally and ethically, and they could be of poor quality, but my focus is on the musical content.

It is possible that misunderstandings regarding "Christian music" are the product of cultural biases. Our "Western ears" are accustomed to certain sounds. Particular modes, scales, and rhythms are part of a rich musical heritage. When we hear music that is not part of that heritage we are tempted to label it, inaccurately, as unfit for a Christian's musical life.

We should realize that music is best understood within its culture. For example, the classical music of India includes quarter tones, which are foreign to our ears. They generally sound very strange to us, and they are often played on instruments, such as the *sitar,* that have a strange sound. But we would be guilty of flagrant prejudice if we were to maintain that such music is non-Christian because it does not contain the tones we are used to hearing. Another example of the way evangelicals tend to misapply the term *Christian* to music can be understood by reflecting on how music may have sounded during biblical and church history. Scholars have begun to demonstrate that the music of biblical history may have been comprised of tonal and rhythmic qualities that were very different from that to which we are accustomed in Western culture.

The attitudes of Martin Luther and John Calvin toward the use of music show a disagreement concerning the truth of a particular Christian style. Charles Garside provides intriguing insights:

> Luther had openly proclaimed his desire to
> use all available music, including the most
> obviously secular, for the worship of the

church. . . . Calvin, to the contrary, now absolutely rejects such a deployment of existing musical resources.[2]

It is obvious that these great men did not agree on the nature of music.

Our musical preconceptions do not die easily, and they seem to recur periodically in church history. Once a style becomes familiar enough, it is accepted. Until then, it is suspect. More recent examples can be found in the controversies surrounding the use of instruments such as drums and guitars during worship services. Evangelicals need to be alert to their biases and understand that "Christian music" is a misnomer.

The "Power" of Music

People often claim that music has "power" to manipulate and control us. If this were true, Skinnerian determinism would be correct in asserting that there is no such thing as personal choice or responsibility. Music, along with other "powers" found in our cultural settings, would be given credit for an influence it does not wield.

Best and Huttar address this issue:

> The fact that music, among other created and cultural things, is purported by primitives and sophisticates alike to have power is more a matter of the dislocation of priorities than anything else.[3]

Such beliefs stimulate not only a "dislocation of priorities" but also poor theology.

The Bible tells us that early in their relationship David played music for King Saul (1 Sam. 16, 18). On one occasion what Saul heard soothed him (1 Sam. 16:23), and on another occasion the same sounds infuriated him (1 Sam. 18:10–11). In reality, though, the reactions were Saul's decisions. He was not passive; he was not being manipulated on either occasion by the "power" of the music.

Much contemporary thinking places the blame for aberrant behavior (sexual misconduct, rebellion, violence, and so on) on the supposed intrinsic potency of music to orchestrate our actions. Some people extend this reasoning to the point of believing that music is the special tool of Satan; when aberrant behavior is exhibited, he is the culprit. Again, Best and Huttar offer pertinent thoughts on this issue:

> Ultimately the Judeo-Christian perspective maintains that man is interiorly wrong and that until he is right he will place the blame for his condition outside himself.[4]

Admittedly, my point is subtle. We must be careful not to imply that music cannot be used for evil purposes. But we must realize that the devil goads people who use music; he does not empower the music itself.

Current controversy among Christians concerning the rhythmic content of rock music is an example of the tendency to believe that some musical styles are intrinsically evil. For example, Steve Lawhead has demonstrated that the music of the early slaves probably did not include much rhythmic substance at all. The plantation owners would not have allowed drums because they could have been used to relay messages of revolt between the groups of slaves.

This observation is central to the issue of rock music, because some people assert that the syncopated rhythm of rock is the product of the pagan African backgrounds of the slaves. In reality, American slave music revolved around the playing of a *banya,* an instrument akin to the banjo, and not drums or other rhythmic instruments.[5]

Rock music is not intrinsically evil. It did not originate in a pagan past, and even if it did that would not mean that it is evil. Nevertheless, since it has been a prominent and influential part of American culture for several decades, it demands the attention of evangelicals. The attention we give it should begin with the understanding that the problems that are a part of rock do not reside in the music itself; they reside in sinful people who can and often do abuse it. The same can be said about any other musical style or art form.

The Quality of Music

So far, I have asserted two propositions concerning how Christians can respond to the music of their culture: the term Christian music is a misnomer, and no musical style is intrinsically evil. Although both of these statements are true, they say nothing about the quality of music we choose to make a part of our lives. Thus, my third proposition is that music should be evaluated based on quality. A proposal that includes judgments of quality is challenging. Evangelicals will find this especially difficult because the subject of aesthetics is not a prevalent part of our heritage.

Evangelicals tend toward lazy thinking when it comes to analyzing the music of their culture. As Frank Gaebelein said, "It is more difficult to be thoughtfully discriminating than to fall back upon sweeping generalization."[6] Several factors must be weighed if discriminating thought is to occur.

We should focus attention on the music within Christian life. This point applies not only to music used in worship but also to music heard via radio, compact disks, concerts, and other sources.

Lack of quality is one of the themes of people who write about contemporary church music. Harold Best states, "Contentment with mediocrity as a would-be carrier of truth looms as a major hindrance to true creative vision among evangelicals."[7] Robert Elmore continues in a similar vein:

> There are even ministers who feed their congregations with the strong meat of the Word and at the same time surround their preaching with only the skimmed milk of music.[8]

If negative declarations such as these are the consensus of those who have devoted ardent attention to the subject, what are the contents of a positive model? The answers to this question are numerous. I will relate only some of the insights of one thinker, Calvin Johansson.

The first insight refers to movement. Music must move. The principle here is that music needs to exhibit a flow, an overall feel for continuity, that moves progressively and irresistibly from beginning to end. It is not intended to hammer and drive a musical pulse into the mind. This principle can be applied to the incessant nature of the rock rhythm we discussed earlier.

The second insight has to do with cohesion. Unity is an

organic pull, a felt quality that permeates a composition so thoroughly that every part, no matter how small, is related.

The third insight relates to "diversions at various levels. . . . Without diversity there would only be sameness, a quality that would be not only boring but also devastatingly static."

The fourth insight focuses on "the principle of dominance. . . . A certain hierarchy of values is adopted by the composer in which more important features are set against the less important."

The fifth insight shows that "every component part of a composition needs to have intrinsic worth in and of itself. . . . The music demonstrates truth as each part of the composition has self-worth."[9]

These principles contain ideas that the nonmusician might find difficult to understand. Indeed, most of us are not accustomed to using language to discuss the quality of the music we hear other than to say that we do or do not "like" it. But if we are going to assess accurately the music of the broader culture, we must be able to use such language to assess music within our own subculture. We must seek quality there.

Pop Music

Another factor in musical discrimination applies to the way we approach music outside our subculture. The Christian is free to enter culture equipped with discernment, and this certainly applies to music. We need not fear the music of our culture, but we must exercise caution.

Assessments of quality also apply here. The Christian should use the principles we discussed earlier to evaluate the music of the broader culture.

We should also be aware of the blending of music and message or the lack of such blending. The ideal situation occurs when both the medium and the message agree.

Too often the music we hear conveys a message at the expense of musical quality. Best explains it thus:

> The kind of mass communication on which the media subsist depends on two things: a minimal creative element and a perspective that sees music only as conveying a message rather than being a message. Viewed as a carrier, music tends to be reduced to a format equated with entertainment. The greater the exposure desired, the lower the common denominator.[10]

The messages of our culture are perhaps voiced most strongly and clearly through music that is subordinated to those messages. The music is "canned." It is the product of musical clichés and "hooks" designed to bring instant response from the listener. As Erik Routley stated, "All music which self-consciously adopts a style is like a person who puts on airs. It is affected and overbearing."[11] This condition is so prevalent in contemporary music that it cannot be overemphasized.

Another concern is found in certain features of what is usually called "popular culture." Music is a major part of pop culture. Kenneth Myers, among others, has identified certain culture types beginning with "high," diminishing to "folk," and plummeting to "popular." Popular culture "has some serious liabilities that it has inherited from its origins in distinctively modern, secularized movements." Generally, these liabilities include "the quest for novelty, and the desire for instant gratification."[12] In turn, these same qualities are found in "pop" music.

The quest for novelty is apparent when we understand, as Steve Lawhead states, that "the whole system feeds on the 'new'—new faces, new gimmicks, new sounds. Yesterday in pop music is not only dead; it is ancient history."[13]

The desire for instant gratification is the result of the fact that this type of music is normally produced for commercial reasons. Continuing, Lawhead writes,

> Commercialism, the effective selling of products, governs every aspect of the popular music industry. From a purely business point of view, it makes perfect sense to shift the focus from artistic integrity to some other less rigorous and more easily managed, non-artistic component, such as newness or novelty. Talent and technical virtuosity take time to develop, and any industry dependent upon a never-ending stream of fresh faces cannot wait for talent to emerge.[14]

We do not offer God our best when we employ this approach. Additionally, we do not honor God when we make the products of such thinking a consistent part of our lives. Let us encourage one another to glorify God through the music that surrounds us.

11

Film and
the Christian

Todd A. Kappelman

An examination of the history of the twentieth century
reveals the importance of viewing and studying film
for any individuals who wish to understand themselves
and their time and place. Film is essential because the
distinction that so many people make between so-called
"high" and "low" culture has in fact disappeared (if it ever
existed in the first place).

The early twentieth century saw the dawn of electronic
technology, beginning with the invention of the radio,
which gave birth to mass media and communications. The
increase in leisure time and wealth fostered the birth and
development of an entertainment industry. The decline in
the quality of education and the explosion in the popularity
of television sealed the union between what was tradi-
tionally considered "high" art and popular culture. The
image, the sound, and the moving picture now define
Western society more strictly than the written word, which
defined previous centuries. Seldom does anyone ask, "What
have you read lately?" One is much more likely to hear
the question, "What have you seen lately?" We have become,
for better or worse, a visually oriented society. Because

literature is no longer the dominant form of expression, scriptwriters, directors, and actors do more to shape the culture in which we live than do the giants of literature or philosophy. We may be at the point in the development of Western culture that the Great Books series needs to be supplemented by a Great Films series.

The church as a body has a long-standing and somewhat understandable tradition of suspicion concerning narrative fiction, the concepts of which apply here to our discussion of film. A brief examination of positions held by some Christians from the past regarding written fictional narratives may help us to understand the concern some people have with involvement in fictional narratives as recorded on film.

Alcuin, an influential Christian leader of the ninth century was extremely concerned about the worldliness he saw in the church. One of the things that troubled him most was the monks' fondness for fictional literature and stories about heroes such as Beowulf and Ingeld. Writing to Higbald, Alcuin said, "Let the words of God be read aloud at the table in your refectory. The reader should be heard there, not the flute player; the Fathers of the Church, not the songs of the heathen. . . . What has Ingeld to do with Christ?"[1]

Tertullian, the father of Latin theology, writing six centuries earlier, voiced a similar concern about Christians involved in secular matters when he asked, "What has Athens to do with Jerusalem?"[2] Specifically, Tertullian believed that the study of pagan philosophers was detrimental to the Christian faith and should be avoided at all costs.

Paul, writing to the church at Corinth, asked, "What partnership does righteousness have with iniquity? Or what fellowship has light with darkness? What accord has Christ with Belial?"[3]

Conclusion: The objections raised against the arts, both past and present, do have merit and should not be dismissed too quickly. Christians have a right and a responsibility to ensure that entertainment and art are not used in a manner that is damaging to their spiritual welfare. It is often a difficult call. For example, many Christians objected to the work of Federico Fellini and Ingmar Bergman in the fifties and sixties, yet men such as Francis Schaeffer thought that it was necessary to pay attention to what these individuals were saying and why.

The Nature of Film and the Opportunity for Christians

Properly understood, film is a narrative medium—a kind of "visual book" with a beginning, middle, and ending —that contains some degree of resolution. All film is not created equal; some movies are made with the express purpose of providing diversionary entertainment whereas others represent the sincere efforts of artists to make works of art that reflect human emotions and call people to a more reflective existence. This second category of film should be considered an art form and is therefore worthy of the same attention that any other art—such as the ballet, sculpture, or painting—receives.

Art is the embodiment of humanity's response to reality and its attempt to order the experience of that reality.[4] People have always expressed and will continue to express, through the arts, their hopes and excitement and their fears and reservations about life, death, and what it means to be human. They will seek to express their world through all available means, and that now includes film. *Schindler's*

List, a film by Steven Spielberg, is an excellent example of film's ability to express hopes and fears.

As a picture of reality, film is able to convey an enormous range of human experiences and emotions. The people one encounters in films are frequently like us, regardless of whether they are Christian. Often the people we see in the better films are struggling with some of the most important questions in life. They are attempting to find meaning in what often appears to be a meaningless universe. These people are often vehicles used by a director, producer, or writer to prompt us to ask the larger questions of ourselves.

Film is not and should not be required to be uplifting or inspiring. Christians should remember that non-Christians also have struggles and wrestle with the meaning of life and their place and purpose in the universe. Christians and non-Christians will not and should not be expected to come to the same conclusion on the problems they face in the fictional universe of film. The Scriptures indicate that Christians and non-Christians are different, and this should be a point of celebration, not alarm, for the Christian audience.

T. S. Eliot, speaking specifically about literature but with much that can be applied to film, had the following advice for the Christian:

> Literary criticism should be completed from a definite ethical and theological standpoint. . . . It is necessary for Christian readers [and film goers by extension], to scrutinize their reading [again, film viewing by extension], especially of works of imagination, with explicit ethical and theological standards.[5]

Therefore, Christians should take their worldview with them when they attend and comment on any film. They should be cautious about judging a film that does not conform to Christian beliefs or their particular notion of orthodoxy as unfit for consumption or undeserving of the right to exist as art.

Conclusion: The need for participation in film arises from, not only the diversity of material with which the medium deals, but also the plurality of possible interpretations concerning a given film. Christians have an opportunity to influence their culture by entering the arena of dialogue provided by film and contending for their positions and voicing their objections with sophistication, generosity, and a willingness to hear from those of opposing beliefs.

Some Concerns About Christian Participation in Cinema

Christians are often concerned about the content of certain films and the appropriateness of viewing particular pieces. This is a valid consideration that should not be dismissed too quickly, and it certainly deserves a response from those who do view objectionable material. The two primary areas of concern leveled by the many detractors of contemporary culture as it pertains to film are found in the categories of gratuitous sex and violence. It is crucial that Christians understand the exact nature of sex and violence, gratuitous and otherwise, and how it may be employed in art. Taking only violence as the representative issue of these two concerns, we must ask ourselves what, if any, redeeming value does it have, and whether it should be used and viewed under some circumstances?

We might turn to the use of gratuitous violence in literature better to understand the role of violence in film. If we can understand and embrace (albeit with reservation) the former, we can also understand and embrace (again, with caution) the latter as a means of expression employed by a new image-driven culture.

The image of gratuitous violence in modern times has one of its first and most important articulations in *The Rime of the Ancient Mariner* by Samuel Taylor Coleridge. Recall that in the poem the sailor shoots an albatross for absolutely no reason and is condemned by his fellow sailors, who believed that the bird was a good omen, to wear the dead body around his neck. The ship is ravaged by plague, and only the cursed mariner survives. After many days of soul-searching on the ghost ship, the mariner pronounces a blessing upon all of creation and atones for his wrongs. A sister ship saves the man, and he begins to tell his story evangelistically to anyone who will listen.

Every time this poem is read in a class or other group, some person invariably is fixated on the act of violence and emphasizes it to the point of losing the meaning of the entire poem. The story is about a mariner who realizes the errors of his ways, repents, and comes to a restored relationship with creation and other men. For Coleridge, the act of violence thus became the vehicle for the turning of the character's soul from an infernal orientation to a paradisaical orientation.

Other authors have used similar methods. Dante, for example, repeated a similar pattern when he explored the spiritual realms in his poetic chronicle *The Divine Comedy*. First, he takes his readers through the harshness, pain, and misery of the Inferno before moving into Purgatory and finally into the bliss and joy of Paradise. Dostoyevsky composed a series of four novels that begins with the heinous crime of Raskolnikov and finishes with the salvation of the Karamazov brothers.

Conclusion: The writers mentioned here and many serious, contemporary filmmakers often explore the darkness of the human condition. They don't do it simply to posture or exploit but to see deeply and lay bare the problems and tensions of life. But they also do it to look for answers, even the light of salvation. The picture is not always pretty, and the very ugliness of the scene is often necessary to portray accurately the degree of depravity and the miracle of salvific turns in fiction. By virtue of their full acquaintance with the dark side of the human condition, the filmmakers are able to propose solutions that appear to be viable and realistic.[6]

Biblical Examples of Gratuitous Violence

The prohibition against and objections to the use of violence in film may be understood better by examining the use of violence in the Bible.

One example found in Scripture is in the thirteenth chapter of the book of Isaiah. In verses 15 and 16 the prophet is forecasting the particulars of the future Assyrian military invasion and the conditions that the people of Israel and the surrounding countries will experience:

> *Whoever is captured will be thrust through; all who*
> *are caught will fall by the sword. Their infants*
> *will be dashed to pieces before their eyes; their houses*
> *will be looted and their wives ravished.*
> (Isa. 13:15–16)

The prophet is talking about the impaling of men by the conquering armies, the willful smashing of infants upon the rocks, and the raping of women. In an oral- and textual-based society, those who heard the words of Isaiah would have been able to imagine the horrors he described and would have made mental images of the scenes.

In an image-driven society, if this scene were to be part of a movie, a scriptwriter and director would have actors and actresses play the parts, and the violence would be obvious to all. Recall the scene in the movie *The Ten Commandments* in which the Egyptian armies attempted to follow Moses across the Red Sea. One sees trapped horses and soldiers under tons of water. Their bodies go limp before they can get to the surface. And those who can make it to the top face certain death trying to swim back to shore. In spite of these, and other horrific scenes, many people deem this movie a "Christian classic" and a good family film.

A second and even more disturbing example of gratuitous violence in the Bible is found in chapters 19 and 20 of Judges. A Levite and his concubine enter the house of an old man from the hill country of Ephraim to spend the night. While they are there, some wicked men in the city want to have homosexual relations with the Levite traveler and demand that the old man hand them over. The evil men take the man's concubine and rape and kill her, leaving her dead body in the doorway. The traveler is so distraught that he cuts his concubine into twelve pieces and sends the body parts back to his fellow Israelites. The Israelites then form a revenge party and go into battle with the Benjamites, who will not turn over the evil men for punishment.

Again, if this story were to be translated into a visual medium, the scenes of rape and later dismemberment of a body, even if they were filmed in standards from the forties or fifties, would be very disturbing.

Conclusion: The purpose of the violence in these examples may be that the details in each passage provide information that is a reason for a later action. Or the information provided shows us something about the nature of God and the way He deals with sin. If both of these examples show a difficult but necessary use of violence in telling a story, then perhaps violence may be used (portrayed) for redemptive purposes in fictional media such as film. This is not an airtight argument; rather, the issue is raised as a matter for consideration while keeping in mind that Christians should always avoid living a vicariously sinful life through any artistic medium.

Weaker Brother Considerations in Viewing Film

Paul's great teaching concerning meat sacrificed to idols and the relationship between the stronger and weaker brothers is discussed in 1 Corinthians 8. We should remember that Paul clearly puts the burden of responsibility on the stronger brother, who should have in mind the interests of the weaker brother.

While some people exercise extreme Christian freedom in watching films that are objectionable to some other people, that fact does not necessarily mean that they are strong Christians. It could indicate that these people are too weak to control their passions and are hiding behind the argument that they are stronger brothers. Do not urge others to participate in something that you, as a Christian, feel comfortable doing if they have reservations. You could inadvertently cause the other person to sin.

Basically, three positions can be taken in relation to Christians' viewing of films.

The first position is prohibition, the belief that films (and often television and other forms of entertainment) are inherently evil and detrimental to the Christian's spiritual well-being. People who maintain this position avoid all films, regardless of the rating or reputed benefits, and they urge others to do the same.

The second position is abstinence, the belief that it is permissible for Christians to view films, but for personal reasons some people choose not to do so. They might abstain for reasons ranging from concern for the use of time, to no real desire to watch a film, to avoidance because it could cause them, or someone about whom they are concerned, to stumble. Willingly abstaining from some or all films does not automatically make one a weaker brother, and we should avoid making such a charge! We should avoid labeling a fellow Christian "weaker" for choosing to abstain from participation in some behavior because it is against his or her conscience.

The third position is moderation, the belief that it is permissible to watch films and that one may do so within a certain framework of moderation. A person taking this position willingly views some films but considers others to be inappropriate for Christians. A great deal of disagreement occurs over what a Christian can or cannot and should or should not watch. Although some of these disagreements are matters of principle and not of taste, we should practice Christian charity whenever we are uncertain.

Conclusion: A valid history of concern exists about Christian involvement in the arts and fictional and imaginative literature. This issue extends to the medium of film.

There are similar concerns about films and Christians who view films. However, because film is one of the dominant means of cultural expression, film criticism is necessary. If Christians do not make their voices heard, then others—often non-Christians—will dominate the discussion. All films contain the philosophical persuasions of the persons who contribute to their development, and it is the job of the Christian who participates in these arts to make insightful, fair, and well-informed evaluations of the work. Not everyone feels comfortable viewing some (or any) films, and the Christian should be especially mindful of the beliefs of others and always have the interests of fellow believers and nonbelievers in mind. Although "film," the artistic expression of the cinematic medium, and not "movies," the entertainment-based expression, has been the focus of this discussion, much of what has been said of the former is applicable to the latter.

Tempering Christian Freedom with Restraint

Christians should be aware that the freedoms exercised in participating in the film arts are privileges. They should not be practiced to the point of vicarious living. In 1 Corinthians 10:23 (and 6:12), the apostle Paul writes that "everything is permissible—but not everything is constructive" (NIV). He is addressing the issue of meat sacrificed to idols in chapter 10 and sexual purity in chapter 6.

This passage can serve both as a guide for Christians who are concerned about their involvement in film and a caution against construing what is written here as a license to watch anything and everything. The apostle is very careful to distinguish between what is permissible, and what is constructive or expedient. Paul means that, in

Christ, believers have freedoms that extend to all areas of life, but these freedoms have the potential to be exercised carelessly or without regard to others, and thus to become sin. The guiding rule here is that Christians should seek the good of others and not their own desires, meaning that anyone who is participating in a film that is objectionable should have the interests of others, both believers and nonbelievers, in mind. We live in a fallen world, and almost everything we touch we affect with our fallen nature, even the arts. If we are to be active in redeeming culture for the glory of God, then we must participate in the culture and be light and salt to a very dark and unsavory world.

Parents who are concerned for the spiritual and psychological welfare of their children would do well to offer more than prohibitions against viewing certain films. As with anything that involves Christian freedom, they must consider the children's maturity in each matter. The example of a young child's first BB gun may serve as an illustration. In some instances, children might be ready for their first air rifle at age twelve or thirteen. Other children might not be ready until they are eighteen, and some might be best served if they never possess the gun in question.

Parents should realize that film is a narrative medium that often contains complex philosophical ideas. To continue to absorb films at the current rate and not offer thoughtful criticism on what we are watching is equivalent to visiting museums and announcing that the Picasso or Rembrandt retrospective is "cool" or "stupid." If we are concerned parents and want to gain the respect of our children, we can and must do better than this.

12

Is It Just Entertainment?

Jerry Solomon

Picture a grocery store in your mind. Its many aisles are filled with a variety of products: fresh fruit, vegetables, canned foods, bread, cereal, meat, dairy products, frozen foods, soap, and numerous other items. When we shop in such a store, we need to be aware of certain things, including the price, size, weight, brand, quality, and freshness of the products. After analyzing all of these factors, we are left with the most important part of the shopping trip—the decision! We must decide which of the products we will buy.

Our world is a lot like a grocery store. A variety of ideas (worldviews) are there for our consideration. We can see and hear those ideas through television, music, movies, magazines, books, billboards, bumper stickers, and various other sources. In a sense, we are shopping in the grocery store of ideas. As Christians, we must be aware of the products. We must consider what is being sold. Then we need to decide if we should make a purchase.

Most of us want to be physically healthy. Unfortunately, sometimes we don't eat as if that were true. The same is true of our minds. We want to be mentally healthy. But too often we don't "eat" as if that were true! Our minds are often filled with things that are unhealthful, especially regarding the entertainment we choose. How can we become more aware of the products and make the right purchases when we "go shopping" in the world of entertainment?

A Christian is usually encouraged to think of God's Word, the Bible, as the guide for life. Of course the challenge of such a position is found in practice, not theory. Living by the tenets of Scripture is not always easy. And we can be tempted to think that God's ideas are restrictive, negative, and life-rejecting. The "don'ts" of biblical teachings can appear to overshadow a more positive, life-affirming perspective.

Does God Intend for Us to Enjoy Life?

Think of a series of three questions. First, if you make the Bible your standard for living, does that mean that life will be dull? Some Christians tend to live as if the answer is "yes," especially as applied to entertainment. It appears that we are to be so separate from the world that we can't enjoy any part of it. Second, if you wrote a song, a poem, or a novel, or if you painted a picture or sculpted a statue, do you think that you would know best how it should be sung, read, or understood? Of course, the answer is "yes." It came from your mind and imagination. You "brought it to life." Third, if God created all things and knows everything about you, do you believe that He knows how to bring true joy into your life? Again, the answer is obviously "yes." You came from His mind and imagination. He "brought you to life." He knows best how you should be "sung," "read," and "understood." And He relays that information through His Word, the Bible. He wants you to enjoy life but with His guidelines in mind.

What Is God's Will for Entertainment?

Just what are those guidelines? What is God's will for us concerning entertainment?

Before we answer this question, it is important for us to understand that the Bible clearly teaches God's will for much of life. Sometimes we try to find God's will in Scripture concerning important issues such as our occupations, marriage partners, and important decisions. The answers are not always clear. On the other hand, the Bible frequently teaches the will of God for daily living in obvious ways. The following passages are examples of this point.

- "A wise man is cautious and turns away from evil, but a fool is arrogant and careless" (Prov. 14:16).
- "Let us behave properly as in the day, not in carousing and drunkenness, not in sexual promiscuity and sensuality, not in strife and jealousy" (Rom. 13:13).
- "Flee immorality" (1 Cor. 6:18a).
- "Finally, brethren, whatever is true, whatever is honorable, whatever is right, whatever is pure, whatever is lovely, whatever is of good repute, if there is any excellence and if anything worthy of praise, let your mind dwell on these things" (Phil. 4:8).
- "See to it that no one takes you captive through philosophy and empty deception, according to the tradition of men, according to the elementary principles of the world, rather than according to Christ" (Col. 2:8).

- "Put them all aside: anger, wrath, malice, slander, and abusive speech from your mouth" (Col. 3:8).
- "Now flee from youthful lusts, and pursue righteousness, faith, love and peace, with those who call on the Lord from a pure heart" (2 Tim. 2:22).

Obviously, various types of contemporary entertainment are not mentioned in these verses. The Bible "does not endeavor to specify rules for the whole of life."[1] Therefore, we are challenged to make decisions about entertainment based upon the application of biblical principles. The Christian must know the "principles for conduct: which apply here, which do not, and why. Then he must decide and act. Thus, by this terrifying and responsible process, he matures ethically. There is no other way."[2] In fact, this process signifies our continual spiritual growth, or sanctification. As Hebrews 5:14 states, "Solid food is for the mature, who because of practice have their senses trained to discern good and evil." Probably most of us don't think of "training our senses," but such a concept surely should be a part of our thinking continually.

Perhaps an illustration from the circus can help to make this point clearer. During a circus performance, the most exciting moment comes when the animal trainer steps into the center ring. Imagine that you are in the audience. You hear the ringmaster ask for your attention. He says something like this: "Ladies and gentlemen, boys and girls, please direct your gaze to the center ring! You will notice the cage is filling with ferocious lions, tigers, and bears (Oh my!). You also will notice that a man is entering the cage. This man has never before done this! He has never entered a cage with these or any other wild animals!" The audience gasps, realizing that they are about to witness a death-defying, foolish feat. Indeed, it would be foolish for anyone to do such a thing without a great deal of preparation. Before a legitimate animal trainer enters the cage, he has spent untold hours training the beasts to respond to his voice, his whip, his whistle, or whatever other devices he might use to issue commands and get the response he seeks.

Your ears, eyes, and touch—your senses—are the wild animals; they are to be trained. You must prepare them to enter life ready for whatever may come.

Years ago, I had an opportunity to demonstrate the need for "trained senses" when I attended a heavy metal rock concert at the invitation of a sixteen-year-old friend. He was a new Christian then, and we were spending a lot of time together. He had entered his new life after years of attachment to a certain popular rock musician who was the main act of the concert.

During the evening the musicians heavily emphasized the themes of sex, drugs, and violence, and the crowd of adolescents and preadolescents was encouraged to respond, and they did. After a while, I asked my friend how Jesus would react to what we heard and saw. His response indicated that for the first time he had begun to think about this form of entertainment—which had been very important to him—with Christian principles in mind.

Perhaps the most succinct statement of Christian ethical principles is found in 1 Corinthians 10:31: "Whether, then, you eat or drink or whatever you do, do all to the glory of God." Can you think of anything more than "whatever" or "all"? These all-encompassing words are to be applied to all of life, including our entertainment choices. My young friend made this discovery that night.

What Types of Entertainment Are Evil?

The answer to this question is not always simple. Perhaps the best response is one that doesn't put too much stress on the medium itself. For example, the rhythm of rock music is not evil; television is not evil; movies are not evil; video games are not evil; novels are not evil, and so on.

Of course, it is possible for some people to claim, for instance, that premarital sex is legitimate entertainment. But the clear admonition of Scripture forbids such activity. And the underlying point is not that sex is intrinsically evil. The one who is engaged in premarital sexual activity is taking what is good and misusing it for evil. So evil does not reside in sex, rock music, television, and so on. Various types of entertainment are conduits for good or evil. People are evil. People who provide entertainment, and people who use it, can abuse it. A basic premise of theology is that humankind has a sin nature. We are prone to abuse all things. As Genesis 8:21 states, "The intent of man's heart is evil from his youth."

What About Content?

So the Christian is free to make entertainment a part of his life with the understanding that evil resides in people, not in forms. But caution and discernment must be applied. We must be alert to the importance of our minds and what they can absorb through entertainment.

Perhaps we need to stop doing some of the things we normally do while listening to music, watching television, and so on, so we can concentrate on the ideas that are entering our minds. We might be amazed at what we'll notice if we take the time to concentrate. For example, an old television commercial says, "Turn it loose! Don't hold back!" We may want to ask what "it" refers to, and we may want to know what is not to be "held back." Such a commercial is a thinly veiled espousal of hedonism, an ancient philosophy that says that pleasure is the ultimate good. Ideas are powerful, and they have consequences, even when they come from something as seemingly innocuous as a television commercial.

Consider the following illustration. Think of your mind as a sponge. A sponge absorbs moisture not unlike the way your mind absorbs ideas. (The difference is that you are making choices whereas the sponge is not.) To remove the moisture, you must squeeze the sponge. If someone were to do the same with your "sponge brain," what would come out? Would you be embarrassed if the Lord were to be present? Biblical teaching says that He is always present. If we honor Him, we'll enjoy life as He intended.

If we are using our minds and thinking Christianly about entertainment we will be more alert concerning content. All entertainment is making a statement. Everything we read, hear, or watch espouses a worldview, or philosophy of life. Movies, for example, can range from the introspective existential comedies of Woody Allen to the euphoric pantheistic conjectures of Shirley MacLaine. We are challenged to respond to such content with our Christian worldview intact.

We must take care of our minds. A battle is taking place in the marketplace of ideas. Entertainment can be seen as one of the battlefields where ideas are vying for recognition and influence. As 2 Corinthians 10:5 states, "We are destroying speculations and every lofty thing raised up against the knowledge of God, and we are taking every thought captive to the obedience of Christ." And Colossians 2:8 warns, "See to it that no one takes you captive through philosophy and empty deception, according to the tradition of men, according to the elementary principles of the world, rather than according to Christ."

What About the Conscience?

We should also consider the place of the conscience. We must be aware of the possibility of defiling our conscience (1 Cor. 8:7). As Paul wrote in 1 Corinthians 6:12, "All things are lawful for me, but not all things are profitable." Believers who cannot visit the world without making it their home have no right to visit it at their weak points.[3] It is the responsibility of each of us to be sensitive to what our consciences are telling us when we encounter those weak points and to respond in a way that honors God.

Thus, I suggest the following three steps to cultivate sensitivity in our consciences.

1. Consider what the conscience is relating *before* the entertainment. Is there something about it that we've heard or seen that brings discomfort? If so, it may be a signal to stay away from it.

2. Consider the conscience *during* the entertainment. If we're already watching and listening, are we mentally and spiritually comfortable? If not, we might need to get away from it. Unfortunately, too often the tendency is to linger too long, and in the process we find that what may have disturbed us previously we now take for granted.

3. Consider the conscience *after* the entertainment. Now that it's over, what are we thinking and feeling? We should be alert to what the Lord is showing us about what we have just made a part of our lives.

What Do Others Say?

In addition to an awareness of the conscience, we can benefit from what others have to say. Perhaps advertising will provide information that will prove helpful before we decide to participate. Frequently, advertisements will tell us things about the content and the intent of the producers. Also, we might find it beneficial to be alert to what friends say. The things we hear from them might indicate warning signs, especially if the friends are Christians who are attempting to apply biblical principles to their own lives. In addition, some objective critics can offer insightful comments. Various ministries around the country, for example, are dedicated to analyzing the latest movies. Others attempt to cover a broader spectrum of entertainment from a Christian perspective. You might benefit from subscribing to their publications.

Of course, this encouragement to consider what others say cannot exempt us from personal responsibility. To rely completely on others is an unhealthy practice that can lead to mental and spiritual stagnation. Each of us must be mentally and spiritually alert to the content of entertainment.

Isn't It "Just Entertainment"?

Maybe you've heard someone say, "It's just entertainment!" Is this statement true?

The principles we have affirmed can elicit this and several other common objections. Our answers to these objections can help us gain additional insight into how we think about contemporary entertainment.

1. Some people say that what has been shown in a movie or some other entertainment is "just reality." But is reality a legitimate guideline for

living? Do we derive an "ought" from an "is"? Saying that reality has been portrayed says nothing about the way things ought to be from God's perspective. Reality requires analysis and often correction.

2. A common statement is, "I'm just killing time." The person who says this might be doing exactly that, but what else is being killed in the process? The Christian redeems time; he doesn't kill it. As Ephesians 5:15–16 states, "Be careful how you walk, not as unwise men, but as wise, making the most of your time, because the days are evil."

3. "It won't affect me" is a common objection. Tragically, these can be the proverbial "famous last words" for some people. Ted Bundy, a serial killer who was executed for his crimes, began to look at pornography when he was very young. If he had been warned of the potential consequences of his actions in those early years, he probably would have said that it wouldn't affect him. But we can't predict the outcome of our actions with absolute clarity. In addition, we might not recognize the consequences when they appear because we have been blinded subtly over a period of time.

4. Other people say, "There's nothing else to do." This is a sad commentary on contemporary life. If that is true, then God has done a poor job of supplying us with imagination. Spending hours watching television each day, for instance, says a great deal about our priorities and the use of our God-given abilities and spiritual gifts.

5. Young people in particular tend to say, "Everybody's doing it." It is highly doubtful that

this argument is true. More importantly, we must understand that God's principles don't rely on democracy. We might be called to stand alone, as difficult as that may be.

6. Some people say, "No one will know." Humanly, this reasoning is absurd. The people who say this know. They're somebody, and they have to live with themselves. And if they are Christians, their worldview informs them that God knows. Are they trying to please God or themselves?

7. "It's just entertainment" can also be a response. No, it's not just entertainment. We can't afford to approach contemporary entertainment with the word "just." Too much is at stake if we care about our minds, our witness, and our future.

So what should we do? Should we become separatists? No, the answer to the challenge of entertainment is not to become secluded in "holy huddles" of legalism and cultural isolation. Should we become consumers? No, not without discernment. As we wrote in the beginning of this chapter, when it comes to entertainment, we should be as selective in that "grocery store of ideas" as we are in the food market. Should we become salt and light? Yes! We are to analyze entertainment with a Christian worldview, and we are to "infect" the world of entertainment with that same vision.

Additional Reading

Henry, Carl F. H. "New Testament Principles of Conduct." In *Christian Personal Ethics*. Grand Rapids: Baker, 1957.

Larsen, David L. *The Company of the Creative: A Christian Reader's Guide to Great Literature and Its Themes*. Grand Rapids: Kregel Publications, 1999.

Lawhead, Stephen R. *Rock of This Age: The Real and Imagined Dangers of Rock Music.* Downers Grove: InterVarsity, 1987.

———. *Turn Back the Night: A Christian Response to Popular Culture.* Westchester: Crossway, 1985.

Medved, Michael. *Hollywood vs. America: Popular Culture and the War on Traditional Values.* New York: Harper Collins Zondervan, 1992.

Myers, Kenneth A. *All God's Children and Blue Suede Shoes: Christians and Popular Culture.* Westchester: Crossway, 1989.

Ryken, Leland, ed. *The Christian Imagination: Essays on Literature and the Arts.* Grand Rapids: Baker, 1981.

Schaeffer, Francis A. *Art and the Bible.* Downers Grove: InterVarsity, 1973.

Schultze, Quentin J., et al. *Dancing in the Dark: Youth, Popular Culture, and the Electronic Media.* Grand Rapids: Eerdmans, 1991.

Schultze, Quentin J. *Redeeming Television.* Downers Grove: InterVarsity, 1992.

13

Television and the Christian

Jerry Solomon

Years ago I witnessed something that has become indelibly etched in my memory. The occasion was a week-long summer conference for high school students on the campus of a major university. I was serving as the leader of one of the groups at this conference. In fact, I was given the elite students. They were described as the "Advanced School" because they had attended the conference before, and they held leadership positions on their respective campuses.

Each of our teaching sessions—which were usually focused on matters of worldviews, theology, cultural criticism, and evangelism—began with music. Before one memorable session the music leader began to play the theme music from various television shows of the past. To my great surprise the students began to sing the lyrics to each of the tunes with great gusto. They were able to respond to each theme without hesitation; the songs were ingrained in their memories. Obviously they had heard the themes and watched the programs numerous times during their relatively young lives. Whether *Gilligan's Island, The Beverly Hillbillies, Green Acres, Sesame Street,* or a host of other television programs, they knew all of them. Whereas many of these bright students did not have a good grasp of biblical content, they had no problem recalling the content of frivolous television programs that were not even produced during their generation.

The Rise and Influence of Television

In a short period of time, television has cemented itself in our cultural consciousness. As you read the following titles of television programs, certain memories will probably come to mind: *The Milton Berle Show, I Love Lucy, The Steve Allen Show, The $64,000 Question, The Millionaire, Leave It to Beaver, Gunsmoke, The Andy Griffith Show, Candid Camera, As the World Turns, The Twilight Zone, Captain Kangaroo, Dallas, Happy Days, Let's Make a Deal, The Tonight Show, Sesame Street, M*A*S*H*, All in the Family, The Cosby Show,* and *Monday Night Football.*

Perhaps you remember a particular episode, a certain phrase, an indelible scene, a unique character, or, like my high school friends, the title tune. These and a litany of other television programs have permeated our lives. It is difficult, if not impossible, to find a more pervasive, influential conduit of ideas and images than television. For a large segment of the population "television has so refashioned and reshaped our lives that it is hard to imagine what life was like before it."[1]

This powerful medium began to gather the attention of the population soon after World War II. "By 1948, the number of stations in the United States had reached 48, the cities served 23, and sales of TV sets had passed sales of radios."[2] But it was not until 1952 ". . . that TV as we know it first began to flow to all sections of the United States."[3] Interest was so intense that "by 1955 about two-thirds of the nation's households had a set; by the end of the 1950s there was hardly a home in the nation without one."[4] And by 1961 "there were more homes in the United States with TV than with indoor plumbing."[5] Such statistics have continued to increase to the point where "99 percent of all households possess at least one TV, and most have two or more."[6] So the middle-to-late twentieth century has seen the development of one of the most dramatic and powerful methods of communication in recorded history.

Can Television Be Redeemed?

As with all other media, the Christian should weigh carefully the use and abuse of television. Some people are quick to call the television an "idiot box" while they continue to watch it endlessly. Others, borrowing from a famous poem by T. S. Eliot, may disparagingly refer to television as a "wasteland." Still others, as with certain evangelists, may claim that television is the most powerful tool yet devised for the spreading of the gospel.[7]

Whether your perception of television is negative or positive, the Christian must understand that the medium is here to stay, and it will continue to have a significant influence on all of us, regardless of whether we like it. And whether we are discussing television or any other media, it is the Christian's responsibility "to maintain an informed, critical approach to all media while joyfully determining how best to use every medium for the glory of God."[8]

No doubt, this is a challenging endeavor because at first glance it might be difficult to picture ways in which television can be used legitimately for God's glory. Perhaps many of us tend to have what may be called the "Michal Syndrome." Michal, King David's wife, rebuked David for dancing before the ark of God. She had concluded that the "medium" of dancing in this manner was shameful.

But Scripture obviously demonstrates that she was the one to be rebuked in that she "had no child to the day of her death" (2 Sam. 6:23). We will do well to heed at least one of the lessons of this story and be cautious if we are tempted to reject television outright as a potentially unredeemable avenue of expression.

This is an important thought in light of the fact that many highly esteemed thinkers have espoused pessimistic analyses of television. For example, Malcolm Muggeridge, the English sage, wrote, "Not only can the camera lie, it always lies."[9] In fairness, we must add that Muggeridge added balance in his critique and even agreed to be interviewed on William Buckley's *Firing Line,* but his skepticism continues to be well chronicled. Jacques Ellul has written in the same vein. In 1985, Neil Postman, another respected critic, wrote an oft-quoted book titled *Amusing Ourselves to Death.* Postman argues that Aldous Huxley's belief that "what we love will ruin us" is a perfect description of television.[10]

More recently, Kenneth Myers, an insightful cultural critic, also has concluded that it is highly doubtful that the medium can be redeemed (that is, brought under the Lordship of Christ and conformed to His teachings).[11] Such gloomy perspectives continue to be expressed by many of those who study media.

On the other hand, many other well-qualified critics have questioned such viewpoints, if not rejected them. Their analyses of television usually are based upon a more optimistic view of technology. Clifford Christians, a communications scholar, writes, "I defend television. Contrary to Postman and Ellul, I do not consider it the enemy of modern society, but a gift of God that must be transformed in harmony with the redeemed mind."[12] Quentin Schultze, another communications scholar, believes that many Christian intellectuals "are comfortable with printed words and deeply suspicious of images, especially mass-consumed images."[13] David Marc, an American Civilization professor, offers a provocative outlook by relating that the "distinction between taking television on one's own terms and taking it the way it presents itself is of critical importance. It is the difference between activity and passivity. It is what saves television from becoming the homogenizing, mono-lithic, authoritarian tool that the doomsday critics claim it is."[14] We must view television with an active mind that responds with a Christian worldview. We are responsible for what television communicates to us.

How Should We Respond to Television?

Obviously, great disparities of opinion exist among those who think about television more than most of us. How can we humbly approach the subject while considering both positions? I propose that we reflect on an answer to this question by examining several facets of a response.

Television and Communication

First, we should remember that, as with many other contemporary forms of communication and entertainment, the Bible does not include explicit advice about television. We are left to investigate applicable passages and gather perspectives based upon our study. Let's consider some of those passages and see if we can discover insights.

Neil Postman relates an intriguing thought regarding the second of the Ten Commandments: "You shall not make for yourself an idol, or any likeness of what is in heaven above or on the earth beneath or in the water under the earth" (Exod. 20:4). Postman's response to this verse is that "it is a strange injunction to include as part of an ethical system unless its author assumed a connection between forms of human communication and the quality of a culture."[15] Postman's statement strongly suggests that the ways in which we communicate significantly influence our lives. He continues by stating that "iconography thus became blasphemy so that a new kind of God could enter a culture."[16]

We have much to consider in such statements. First, it is true that the "author" (in this case, God via the personality of Moses) was emphasizing the importance of "forms of communication." But it is a misapplication of the text to conclude anything more than that it is not permissible for man to form visual images of God. Second, it is also true that "forms of communication" are connected to the "quality of a culture." But again it is a misapplication to conclude that visual images cannot be a positive or beneficial part of that quality. Third, it is not true that "iconography thus became blasphemy" for the people of God. If that were so, it would make a mockery of the tabernacle and the temple, which were so important in the cultural and religious life of the Israelites (in particular, see Exodus 31, 35–40). Both structures contained icons that were representative of God's revelation, and they were filled with images that were pleasing to the eye. There was an aesthetic dimension. Of course the icons were not representative of God Himself, but they were representative of His actions and commands. They symbolized God's presence and power among His people.

The point of this dialogue with Postman and his analysis of the second commandment is that he has exhibited one of the most prominent biases against television, that is, that television is an image-bearer and, as such, is inferior to forms of communication that are word-bearers. Even if we were to concede that this bias is true, it does not follow that the inferiority of television means that it cannot be a legitimate form of communication. It simply means that it might be inferior to other forms. Steak might be superior to hamburger, but that doesn't mean that steak should be our only food.

Let's reverse the emphasis upon the superiority of written communication by considering a contrast between reading the letters of the apostle Paul and actually being in his presence and hearing him expound upon them. Most of us would probably say that actually hearing Paul is superior to reading him, but few of us would say that reading his letters is not a worthwhile enterprise. If we follow the reasoning of Postman and the other critics, we might be tempted to conclude that the issue of inferiority/superiority could lead us to reject reading Paul because that does not provide the same level of communication as would his actual presence. Television might be inferior to other things in our lives, but that doesn't mean that we must exclude it.

The Cultural Mandate and Television

Second, we should analyze television in light of the cultural mandate. Clifford Christians related that Christians "often seem to be aliens in a strange land." That is, we are living in a secularized society that makes it increasingly difficult to assert biblical principles. But he goes on to draw a parallel between the ancient Israelites in their Babylonian captivity and our present condition. He quotes the prophet Jeremiah:

> *"Build houses and live in them; and plant gardens,*
> *and eat their produce. . . . And seek the welfare of the*

city where I have sent you into exile, and pray to the
LORD on its behalf; for in its welfare you will have
welfare. . . . For I know the plans that I have
for you," declares the LORD, "plans for welfare
and not for calamity to give you a future and a hope."
(Jer. 29:5, 7, 11)

This passage can remind us that we are to "convert cultural forms, not eliminate them wholesale."[17] The Israelites were forced to live in a culture that was not their own, but they were still enjoined to "cultivate" it. In the same sense, we should be cultivating the medium of television.

Television Is Still in Its Childhood

Third, we should think about the fact that television is still in its childhood. As a result, it is possible that it has not yet realized its potential beyond the banalities that we now tend to associate with it. A study of the history of various media indicates that all of them have proceeded through stages of development. For example, even though drama was born in ancient Greece, its development had to wait to a great extent until Shakespeare and the Elizabethan era, during which the theater began to acquire its present form. Many people were outraged. In the opinion of the learned and the pious, it was a suspicious and inferior form of communication. This manner of communication or entertainment led the London city fathers to eliminate it from the city and force it into the suburbs. Thus, the famous Globe theater was built on the south side of the Thames and not inside the walled city.[18]

So, it could be that many of us, like the London city fathers, are too impatient, or we are biased. We often cry that there is reason to be impatient or biased because of the television content that has become so much a part of our lives. Yes, television includes too much violence, sex, and secularism, and it has too many vapid plots and too much insipid dialogue. But our concerns about content should not lead us automatically to assume that the medium is irredeemable. Perhaps we have not allowed television the time it needs to attract its most creative and redeeming champions. And again, this is where the Christian should enter armed with the cultural mandate. The Christian who seeks to communicate through television should understand its peculiarities and surpass the unimaginative, superficial, narcissistic productions offered by too many contemporary Christians.

Television and Visual Literacy

Fourth, we should consider the possibility that many of us are visually illiterate, just as the disciples of Jesus were frequently "parable illiterate." We might need to learn how to react to television. This view might sound strange since such a great percentage of the population spends so much time with television. Unfortunately, most of us don't "view" television. Instead, we "watch" television. That is, we don't often engage in a mental, much less a verbal, discussion with the images and dialogue.

The critical viewer of television has the difficult job of translating the tube's images into words. Then the words can be processed by the viewer's mind by being evaluated and discussed with other viewers. All Christians must engage in this crucial process if they hope to be discerning users of television.[19]

Much of current television is designed to appeal to the emotions as opposed to the intellect. The frenetic style of Music Television (MTV), for example, is used increasingly for everything from commercials to news programs. Unless we want to leave television as a medium that applies only to our emotions, we must find ways to interact intellectually with what television delivers. Perhaps more importantly, we must encourage a new generation to become visually literate to the point where they will begin to affect the use of the medium.

Good Decisions About Television

Fifth, many of us should make decisions before we spend time with the medium. We should do this not only for ourselves but also for our children and grandchildren. Perhaps a good rule for turning on the tube is to "map out" what might be worthy of our attention each day. Of course, this means that we will have to spend a few minutes reading what is available. But surely this will prove to be beneficial. Instead of automatically activating the power switch as part of a daily routine regardless of what may be "on" at the time, we will use selectivity.

Television is with us and will continue to exert its influence in ways that are difficult to predict now. The proliferation of cable television, the increasing interest in satellite systems, and the unfolding of futuristic technology, virtual reality, and a host of other developments will probably force us to give even more attention to television than we have heretofore.

So as Christians it appears that we will continue to have the same dilemma: Do we reject the medium or do we redeem it? Because we are called to glorify God in all that we do, it appears that we should not leave watching television out of this mandate. Let us commit ourselves to the redemption of television.

Is Being Touched by an Angel Enough?

Don Closson

D uring a 1997 television ratings week, a relatively new program at the time, *Touched by an Angel,* ranked third with a 16.6 Neilsen rating. That number means that more than sixteen million households were tuned in to watch three angels communicate God's love and offer of eternal life to people in various difficult real-life situations. Also, *TV Guide* magazine featured a special report called "God and Television" that included an article by Jack Miles, author of *God: A Biography.* The article quoted popular writers James Redfield, author of *The Celestine Prophecy;* Rabbi Harold Kushner, author of *When Bad Things Happen to Good People;* Jack Canfield, coauthor of *Chicken Soup for the Soul;* and others.[1] One might conclude that television had suddenly found God, and to a degree that conclusion is right.

Society's Interest in Spirituality

Television producers are discovering that typical television watchers are hungry for programming that includes spiritual themes. In *TV Guide's* own national telephone poll, they discovered that 56 percent of adults think that religion does not get enough attention on prime-time television; only 8 percent think that it gets too much. Of those who responded, 61 percent desired more references to God, church attendance, and other religious observances; 68 percent were eager to see more spirituality as long as it was not tied to organized religion; and 82 percent wanted more emphasis on moral issues. One of the most successful programs at attracting these viewers has been *Touched by an Angel*.

Although it had a rough beginning and was almost canceled, the program made a strong recovery after a professing Christian was hired as executive producer and the focus of the program was changed to more mature topics. The stories revolve around the activities of three angels played by Della Reese, Roma Downey, and John Dye. In the words of the *TV Guide* article, "Never has prime-time network entertainment presented God in such an unabashed and earnest fashion."[2] Recent programs have dealt with death in a sophisticated manner, relating how these angels help humans confront both mortality and the existence of a loving God. Significant topics such as the nature of God, works, eternal destiny, and faith itself have entered into the dialogue. In the words of executive producer Martha Williamson, "our show is God's truth," which is that "God exists. God loves us. God wants to be part of our lives." Della Reese adds, ". . . he has a plan."[3]

Recently, the three actors and their producer were on the Oprah Winfrey show, where they remarked about the popularity of *Touched by an Angel*. The actors have received thousands of letters relating how the program has changed viewers' lives by making spiritual reality more plausible and by focusing on the love of God. The actors are very proud of how they are portraying God. In the words of

John Dye, who plays the angel of death, "If we're doing it poorly, I just don't think God would bless the show and allow it to continue."[4]

Are we experiencing a cease-fire in the culture war? Is the Christian right winning the battle for the media? Some people might argue that only the most cynical observer could find something wrong with programs that promote a loving, personal God who wants a relationship with us and is concerned about our salvation. Let's consider what is good and not so good about programs such as *Touched by an Angel.*

Audience Response

This development of new television programs that are using God-talk during prime-time hours and getting good ratings is a new phenomenon. *Promised Land, Seventh Heaven,* and especially *Touched by an Angel* are going boldly where no producer would have gone before in the spiritual realm. With shows about angels, spirits, and ministers, it might be suggested that television is changing for the better. Maybe the networks are finally listening to the public's demand for programming that is more family oriented and morally uplifting.

In fact, I believe that they are. Although they are not perfect, the new programs are providing a positive service to the viewing community. Let me explain why. Christians have been decrying for years what Richard John Neuhaus called the "naked public square" in a book by the same name.[5] We have lamented the fact that public institutions such as government, education, and the media rarely leave room for a spiritual reality. Naturalism, as a worldview, has had a monopoly. Christianity, if referred to, was ridiculed and parodied—what I like to call the "Frank Burns" form of Christianity. Frank Burns, the character from *M*A*S*H,* was hypocritical, emotionally weak, and possibly dangerous when given any real authority.

Current programming such as *Touched by an Angel* offers a worldview competing with naturalism. It lends plausibility to the notion that there is a loving, personal God. Although the angels seem to struggle somewhat with their own understanding of God's will, they are performing, in a general sense, the most prominent role of angels in Scripture, that of being messengers from God.

The audience also gets a reasonable picture of what life might be like if a spiritual reality is taken seriously. Contrary to the prevailing naturalistic hopelessness that pervades much of our culture, *Touched by an Angel* does offer hope via a relationship with the Creator of the universe. Characters in the episodes are encouraged to seek God and have a relationship with Him. And importantly, they are told that they will not earn salvation by following a set of rules. People in the show are generally treated as complex individuals with weaknesses and strengths, and they respond to life's tragedies in a fairly realistic manner. All of these factors contribute to a positive influence that other networks should be encouraged to emulate. As Christians, we are quick to condemn the negative aspects of television but slow to admit when something positive occurs. This type of programming, which in many ways reminds me of how God would have been expressed or talked about on television in the late 1950s or early 1960s, is a bright spot amid shows such as *Buffy the Vampire Slayer* or *Pacific Palisades.*

But while the program does promote belief in God and the legitimate place that faith should play in one's daily affairs, it falls short in a number of significant ways from being all that Christians would like to see in a bold presentation of biblical truth. Its most glaring omission is the "J" word, as in Jesus Christ. Also, although God is portrayed as loving and caring, little is said about His other attributes such as His holiness and righteousness. *Touched by an Angel* might be a useful springboard from which to present the biblical plan of salvation, but its message is too shallow to be depended upon to evangelize the viewing public on its own. Let's take a closer look at the ways in which *Touched by an Angel* might be a handicap to saving faith for its many fans.

The Nature of God and the Nature of Man

In our look at the return of God to prime-time TV programming, particularly in the *Touched by an Angel* series, we have thus far considered the positive aspects; now we will focus on how it might be improved.

Although *Touched by an Angel* points to a personal God, encourages a personal relationship with that God, and even teaches that our good works are not enough to establish that relationship, it still falls short of teaching a specifically Christian message because of one glaring omission: it never offers a means for that personal relationship. In theological terms, the program never tells us how we are to be found righteous before a holy God. The Bible teaches a concept known as justification which explains how God, being perfectly holy, can declare us righteous enough to enter His presence. The angels on television assume that God will accept us on our own merit; simply turning to Him will bridge whatever separation exists.

This lack of clarity could be the result of a number of factors. The writers might think that there is no need for justification, either because God isn't holy or because mankind isn't sinful or fallen in the biblical sense. Both of these ideas are popular today. Although people might accept the biblical teaching that God is love, they often ignore the equally important truth that God is just and holy. Most portrayals of human nature identify lack of education as the source of our problems, not a sinful nature.

If God is loving but not righteous, then the apostle Paul is in great error when he says in Romans 2:5 that "because of your stubbornness and your unrepentant heart, you are storing up wrath against yourself for the day of God's wrath, when his righteous judgment will be revealed" (NIV). And concerning human nature, he adds that "all have sinned and fall short of the glory of God" (Rom. 3:23 NIV). This great chasm between man and God is an organic part of the Christian gospel and is missing in much of television's current focus on spirituality.

On what basis can people have fellowship with a holy God? If you assert that God is merely a projection of human attributes, He is neither holy nor a real spiritual being. If all of us are God, as New Age pantheists often teach, all we need to do is realize our "godness" via meditation. However, since Jesus walked on the earth, He has been the hope of many in their quest to close the gap between man and God. People have had many different ideas about what Jesus' life accomplished. Some people see His life as an example to be copied. Others accept Paul's teaching in Romans 3, that is, that Jesus provides righteousness from God through his death on the cross, apart from living according to the Jewish law.

But again, confusion exists about who Jesus is. Mormons teach that Jesus was a pre-mortal, as we were at one time, and that everyone can become gods like He is now. Jehovah's Witnesses believe that Jesus' death atoned for the sins of Adam, but that Jesus was an angel who lived a sinless life in the form of humanity. They also insist that good works are necessary to please Jehovah.

These different views cannot all be true. In spite of the good that shows such as *Touched by an Angel* might accomplish, they allow for all such views to be seen as equally valid. When asked in an interview which God (Christian, Jewish, or Muslim) they are representing on the show, Della Reese responded that they talk about a Supreme Being, not about religion. But one has to ask, "Which Supreme Being?"

Sin and Salvation

We turn now to determine which Supreme Being these programs refer to. When *Touched by an Angel* actress Della Reese argues that her program refers to a Supreme Being, not to a religion, just what does she mean?

Della Reese, whose television character Tess was chosen in a *TV Guide* survey as the person most parents would like to be their children's Sunday school teacher, is the pastor of a metaphysical congregation on the west side of Los Angeles where she participates in the "New Thought Movement." The New Thought movement describes itself as "creedless," and it "celebrates individual freedom" but not freedom from acting ethically. Cult leader Barbara Marx Hubbard and author Marianne Williamson (of the *Course in Miracles* fame) recently attended a conference with Ms. Reese, the eighty-first annual meeting of the International New Thought Alliance.[6] We mention all of this not to condemn Ms. Reese or to deny her the right to support the New Thought movement but merely to observe that she is anything but a neutral portrayer of God's nature and activities.

To claim that one can speak the truth about God and do so from a creedless perspective is disingenuous. People who claim knowledge about God must also tell us how they came by this knowledge. If they reject revelation or the Christian creed that results from the Bible, where do they get their information and why should we accept it? Has God spoken to them personally? Are they accepting revelation from another source? How do they know what they proclaim to know about God? They must also tell us why their approach to having a relationship with God is the right one. Even if they hold to the view that all paths lead to God, or that all religious perspectives are valid, we must ask why they believe that is true and why it is an appropriate way to think about God and salvation.

Having said all of that, Christians can use *Touched by an Angel* as a beginning point in talking about God and salvation from a Christian perspective. But the Christian will begin with the message that humanity is fallen and in need of atonement and justification. At the very beginning of Jesus' ministry, John the Baptist said of Him, "Behold, the Lamb of God, who takes away the sin of the world!" (John 1:29). This brief sentence is filled with profound implications. Jesus is both the victim and the priest, both the sacrificial lamb and the high priest who offers the sacrifice. The sacrificial system of the Old Testament taught the necessity of a blood sacrifice as payment for sin. Christ's sacrifice was the once-for-all payment for sin against a holy God. Paul says that we are now justified by Jesus' blood and that He has reconciled to Himself all things, making peace by the blood of His cross (Rom. 3:25; Eph. 2:13). Jesus' death was an act of propitiation. In other words, it removed God's wrath against sinful humans; it appeased His anger. It was also a substitutionary death; He died on our behalf and, in doing so, bore our sins Himself.

These are the truths of Scripture that the new television programs leave out by not mentioning the "J" word. Without Jesus in the picture, being "touched by an angel" still leaves us as sinners before an angry God.

The Gospel and the Great Commission

Finally, we must consider whether programs such as *Touched by an Angel* can be used to share the gospel of Jesus Christ.

In 1 Corinthians 15:1–2, Paul reveals concisely what the Christian gospel is and its significance to believers. He writes, "Now, brothers, I want to remind you of the gospel I preached to you, which you received and on which you have taken your stand. By this gospel you are saved, if you hold firmly to the word I preached to you. Otherwise, you have believed in vain" (NIV). Paul is serious about what is and is not the gospel.

Paul continues by teaching that the gospel is "that Christ died for our sins according to the Scriptures, that he was buried, that he was raised on the third day." Paul then notes that Christ appeared to Peter, the disciples, five hundred believers, James, then to all the apostles, and finally to Paul himself. To Paul, belief in the atoning death of Christ and His resurrection is necessary for salvation.

What Paul claims to be the gospel of Christianity is missing entirely from today's spiritually centered programming. As good as programs such as *Touched by an Angel* are in contrast to the rest of television's weekly fare, they fall far short of giving viewers what they need to know to experience a relationship with God. The God of these programs is enigmatic. We know that He exists, but how we can experience His love and forgiveness is obscure.

But we should be neither surprised nor angry about this situation. Instead, these programs offer great stepping stones to serious discussions about spirituality and the Christian gospel. Evangelism depends upon the common ground that all humans share, including questions about God, fear of death and suffering, alienation, and other topics that are highlighted by these programs. To take advantage of these stepping stones, believers must get beyond the temptation to see Christianity as just another personal enrichment program or self-esteem therapy.

Fallen human beings are unable to satisfy God's judgment and wrath against sin. In this sense, we are depraved. We are not as bad as we could be; that would be absolute depravity. But we are completely unable to please God by our good works. As Isaiah wrote, "All of us have become like one who is unclean, and all our righteous acts are like filthy rags" (64:6). Paul, writing to the church at Ephesus, states, "For it is by grace you have been saved, through faith—and this not from yourselves, it is the gift of God—not by works, so that no one can boast" (Eph. 2:8–9 NIV). If it were not for God's imputing, or attributing, Christ's righteousness to us when we placed our faith in His sacrificial death on the cross, we would have no hope for eternal fellowship with God, regardless of how many angels have touched us.

Network television should be applauded for recognizing and responding to the public's desire for programs that deal with important moral and spiritual themes. However, Christians cannot become complacent or believe that television will now bring about the Great Commission. As always, that job is to be accomplished by spirit-filled ambassadors for Christ who teach the gospel as revealed by Jesus Christ and His apostles.

15

Slogans
Jerry Solomon

L et's try an experiment. I'll list several slogans, some from the past, others from more contemporary times, but I'll leave out one word or phrase. See if you can supply the missing word or phrase. Here are some examples:

- "Give me liberty or give me . . ."
- "Uncle Sam wants . . ."
- "I have a . . ."
- "Ask not what your country can do for you; ask . . ."
- "Just do . . ."
- "Life is a sport; . . ."
- "Gentlemen prefer . . ."
- "Image is . . ."
- "Coke is . . ."
- "You've come a long way, . . ."
- "This is not your father's . . ."
- "You deserve a break . . ."

Well, how did you fare with my experiment? Unless you've been living in a cave for many years, you probably were able to complete several of these phrases. They have become a part of "the fabric of our. . . ." Yes, the fabric of our lives. In most cases, these slogans have been written to promote a product. They are catchy, memorable maxims that help the listener or reader associate the statement with a commodity, thus leading to increased sales. Advertisers spend millions of dollars for such slogans, an indicator of their importance.

Double Meanings

Often a slogan contains a *double entendre,* intended to attract us on at least two levels. For example, an ad for toothpaste from several years ago asked, "Want love?" Obviously, the advertiser is playing upon a universal need. All of us want love. But the initial answer to the question is "Get . . . Close Up." Of course, a couple is pictured in close embrace with vibrant smiles and sweet breath as a result of their wise use of the product. The implication is that they are sharing love, but only as a result of using the love-giving toothpaste. Another example, again from several years in the past, stated, "Nothing comes between me and my Calvins." The double meaning is obvious, especially when the slogan is coupled with the accompanying picture of a young girl. No doubt the companies that hired the ad agencies for such campaigns were very pleased. Their sales increased. The fact that I am even using these illustrations is indicative of their success in capturing the attention of the consumers.

Slogans and the Christian

But the marketplace is not the only arena where slogans are found. Christians often use them. Many contemporary churches strive to attract the surrounding population by using various adjectives to describe themselves. For example, words such as *exciting, dynamic, friendly,* or *caring* are used as part of a catchy slogan designed to grab the attention of anyone who will see or hear it. And such slogans are supposed to describe how that particular church wants to be perceived. This applies especially to congregations that are sometimes called "seeker sensitive." The idea is that there is a market for what is being offered. The surrounding culture will be attracted by the implications of the slogan. One of the foundational tenets of our ministry at Probe is that the Christian should think God's thoughts after Him. Then, the transformed Christian should use his mind to analyze and influence the world around him. One of the more intriguing ways we can experience what it means to have a Christian mind is by concentrating on the content of the slogans we hear and see each day. In this chapter, we will examine certain slogans to discover the ideas imbedded in them. Then we will explore ways we might apply our discoveries to the culture that surrounds us.

Slogan Themes: Vanity

> "Break free and feel; it reveals to the world just how
>   wonderful you are."
> "Spoil yourself."
> "Turn it loose tonight; don't hold back."
> "You deserve a break today."
> "Indulge yourself."
> "Have it your way."

These slogans are indicative of one of the most common emphases in our culture: vanity. The individual is supreme. Selfishness and self-indulgence too often are the primary indicators of what is most important. Such phrases, which are the result of much thought and research among advertisers, are used to play upon the perceptions of a broad base of the population. A product can be promoted successfully if it is seen as something that will satisfy the egocentric desires of the consumer.

Christopher Lasch, an insightful thinker, has titled his analysis of American life *The Culture of Narcissism*. Lasch has written that the self-centered American "demands immediate gratification and lives in a state of restless, perpetually unsatisfied desire."[1] We will return to the subject of immediate gratification later, but the emphasis of the moment is that slogans often focus on a person's vanity. Individuals are encouraged to think continually of themselves, their desires, their frustrations, and their goals. And the quest that is developed never leads to fulfillment. Instead, it leads to a spiraling sense of malaise because the slogans point only to material, not spiritual, ends.

One of the most famous slogans in the Bible is "Vanity of vanities! All is vanity." This exclamation is found in Ecclesiastes, an Old Testament book full of application to our subject. King Solomon, the writer, has left us with an ancient but very contemporary analysis of what life is like if self-indulgence is the key. His analysis came from personal experience. He would have been the model consumer for the slogans that began this essay today: "Break free and feel." "Spoil yourself." "Turn it loose." "You deserve a break today." "Indulge yourself." But he learned that such slogans are lies. As Charles Swindoll wrote,

> In spite of the extent to which he went to find happiness, because he left God out of the picture, nothing satisfied. It never will. Satisfaction in life under the sun will never occur until there is a meaningful connection with the living Lord above the sun.[2]

Solomon indulged himself physically and sexually; he experimented philosophically; he focused on wealth. None of these things fulfilled his deepest needs.

So what is Solomon's conclusion regarding those needs? He realizes that we are to "fear God and keep His commandments, because this applies to every person" (Eccl. 12:13). How would the majority of this country respond if a slogan such as "Fear God and keep His commandments!" were suddenly to flood the media? It probably wouldn't sell very well; it wouldn't focus on our vanity.

One of the Lord's penetrating statements concerning vanity was focused on the man who is called the rich young ruler. Douglas Webster stated,

> It is sad when Jesus is not enough. We are told that Jesus looked at the rich young ruler and loved him. But the love of Jesus was not enough for this man. He wanted it all: health, wealth, self-satisfaction and control. He knew no other way to see himself than the words we use to describe him: a rich young ruler.[3]

Perhaps this analysis can apply to us too often. Is Jesus enough, or must our vanity be satisfied? That's a good question for all of us.

Slogan Themes: Immediate Gratification

"Hurry!"
"Time is running out!"
"This is the last day!"
"You can have it now! Don't wait!"

These phrases are indicators of one of the more prominent themes found in slogans: instant gratification. This is especially true in much of contemporary advertising. The consumer is encouraged to respond immediately. Patience is not a virtue. Contemplation is not encouraged.

Not only do we have instant coffee, instant rice, instant breakfast, and a host of other instant foods but also we tend to see all of life from an instant perspective. If you have a headache, it can be cured instantly. If you need a relationship, it can be supplied instantly. If you need a new car, it can be bought instantly. If you need a god, it can be provided instantly. For example, a few evening hours spent with the offerings of television show us sitcom dilemmas solved in less than half an hour, upset stomachs relieved in less than thirty seconds, and political candidates accepted or rejected based upon paid political announcements. About the only unappeased person on television is the "I love you, man!" guy who can't find a beer or love.

You're a consumer. Be honest with yourself. Haven't you been enticed to respond to a slogan that implies immediate gratification? If you hear or see a slogan that says you must act now, your impulse may lead you to buy. At times, it can be difficult to resist the temptation of the moment. The number of people in serious debt may be a testimony to the seriousness of this temptation. The instant credit card has led to instant crisis because of a thoughtless response to an instant slogan. When we hear "Act now!" or "Tomorrow is too late!" we can be persuaded if we are not alert to the possible consequences of an unwise decision.

One of the most respected virtues is wisdom. The wise man or woman is held in high esteem. This is especially true for the Christian. The Bible tells us of the lives of many people, some of them wise and some of them unwise.

The wise person is portrayed as someone who patiently weighs options, seeks God's counsel, and makes decisions that extend far beyond instantaneous results. The unwise person is portrayed as someone who acts without sufficient thought, doesn't seek God's counsel, and makes decisions that may satisfy for the moment but not in the future. So contemporary Christians should strive to become wise in the face of the slogans that surround them. They should realize that the supposed benefits of products cannot be compared to wisdom. As Scripture states,

> *How blessed is the man who finds wisdom, and the*
> *man who gains understanding. For its profit is better*
> *than the profit of silver, and its gain than fine gold.*
> *She is more precious than jewels; and nothing*
> *you desire compares with her.*
> (Prov. 3:13–15)

Let's develop our own slogan. Perhaps something like, "Wisdom now; decisions later!" would be a good antidote to the messages we hear and see so often. Also, let's implant the fruit of the Spirit in our lives, especially patience and self-control (Gal. 5:22–23). And let's reinforce our thought life with the truth that things of value are not achieved instantly. That reminds me of another slogan: "Rome was not built in a day." And how Rome was built is not nearly as valuable as how our lives are built.

Slogan Themes: Materialism

In the early sixteenth century, an Augustinian monk declared, *Sola Fide!*—"Faith Alone!"—a slogan that had been used by many people before him. But Martin Luther issued this proclamation in opposition to certain theological and ecclesiastical emphases of his time. Instead of teaching that faith could "make" one righteous, he insisted that only God can "declare" one to be righteous based upon Christ's victory on the cross. Eventually, he came to believe that the church needed reformation. And as the saying goes, "The rest is history."

In our time, the most important slogan seems to be *Sola Carnalis,* "The flesh alone!" or "The physical alone!" Put in another way, it is "What you see is what you get!" Material things are usually the focus of our attention. Nonmaterial, or spiritual, things generally are not part of our consciousness. The impression is that life can be lived properly through the purchase of products. Or life is to be lived as if this is the only one you've got; there is no heaven or hell, no sin, no sacrifice for sin, and no judgment. As the old commercial says, "You only go around once in life, so grab for all the gusto you can get." And the slogan of a more recent commercial relates, "It doesn't get any better than this!" as friends share the events of a wonderful day together in a beautiful setting while drinking the right beer. Of course, there is a measure of truth in each of these slogans. We should live life with gusto, and we should enjoy times of companionship with friends. But from a Christian standpoint, these ideas should be coupled with a sober understanding that this life is not all there is.

Jesus often spoke directly to those who would deter Him from His mission, which required His brutal sacrifice. For example, Satan sought to tempt Jesus with material things. But the Lord rejected Satan's enticements by focusing on things that transcend this life. And His rejections always began with a powerful, eternally meaningful slogan: "It is written," a reference to the truth of Scripture. On another occasion, after Jesus showed "His disciples that

He must go to Jerusalem, and suffer many things," Peter proclaimed, "This shall never happen to You." Jesus replied that Peter was setting his mind on man's interests, not God's. Then followed a haunting statement that has become a crucial slogan for those who would be Christ's disciples: "If any one wishes to come after Me, let him deny himself, and take up his cross, and follow Me." This conversation concluded when Jesus asked two rhetorical questions: "For what will a man be profited, if he gains the whole world, and forfeits his soul? Or what will a man give in exchange for his soul?" (Matt. 16:21–26).

Do those questions sound trite? Have we heard and read them so often that we don't consider their implications? If we are immersed in the concepts of today's slogans, such questions should be sobering. Think of our previous examples. Jesus' questions contain answers that say, "No, it is not true that 'You only go around once.' And yes, it does get better than this." We are more than physical beings destined for dirt. We are spiritual and physical beings destined for life in heaven or hell. And for the believer in Christ, this life is to be lived with "the life to come" in mind.

Are We Slaves of Slogans?

"Remember the Alamo!"
"No taxation without representation!"
"I shall return!"
"I have not yet begun to fight!"
"Never give up!"

These memorable slogans are the stuff of legends. They represent a level of commitment that led many people to give their lives for a cause or a country. Are the slogans of today any less intense? No doubt many new slogans are entering the consciousness of those who have been at the center of the tragic conflicts around the world. Strife seems to create powerful slogans.

But what of the strife that is found on the battlefield of our minds? Slogans are indicative of the war that is a part of the life of the mind. (It is fascinating to note that the etymology of the word *slogan* stems from the Gaelic *slaugh-garim,* which was a war cry of a Scottish clan.)

No doubt I could be accused of exaggerating the impact of slogans. But let's remember that enormous amounts of money are spent to encourage us to respond to the messages they contain. For example, commercials shown during the 1998 Super Bowl cost the sponsors approximately one million dollars for a sixty-second spot. Such sums surely would not be spent without a significant payoff. And it is not as if slogans are hidden in some underground culture; we are flooded with them at every turn. As one writer has put it, "Commercial messages are omnipresent, and the verbal and visual vocabulary of Madison Avenue has become our true *lingua franca.*"[4] We might be at the point where we can communicate with one another more readily through the use of advertising slogans because they provide a common ground. But what is that common ground? Is it compatible with a Christian worldview? The answer in our secularized culture is usually "No!"

Our *Lingua Franca*

We have emphasized three themes that are readily found in contemporary slogans: vanity, immediate gratification, and materialism. Of course, slogans include many more subjects, but these three demonstrate that the *lingua franca,* the current common ground, is one that we should weigh carefully against the precepts of Scripture. The Christian worldview cannot accept such themes.

A disciple of Christ is challenged to consider the implications of slogans not only in the marketplace but also in
the church. We can be swayed by the same ideas that drive
those who formulate the slogans of commercialism. Douglas
Webster offers the following penetrating comments.

> Public opinion has become an arbiter of
> truth, dictating the terms of acceptability
> according to the marketplace. The sover-
> eignty of the audience makes serious,
> prayerful thinking about the will of God
> unnecessary, because opinions are formed
> on the basis of taste and preferences rather
> than careful biblical conviction and thought-
> ful theological reflection. Americans easily
> become "slaves of slogans" when discernment
> is reduced to ratings.[5]

Surely none of us would like to be described as a "slave
of slogans." We want to believe that we are capable of
sorting out the messages we hear so often. Yes, we are
capable through the Lord's guidance. But as Webster has
written, we must be sober enough to ensure that taste and
preferences are not leading us. Instead, we should implant
careful biblical conviction and thoughtful theological
reflection in our lives. And I hasten to add that such
thinking should apply to us both individually and within
our churches.

Perhaps the most fitting way to conclude our discussion
of slogans is with another slogan: "To God be the glory in
all things!" Such a thought, if made the center of our lives,
surely will demonstrate the power of slogans.

16

The Games We Play

Jerry Solomon

Ten seconds remain in the game. The Wolves lead by two points. The Bobcats cross midcourt, knowing that they must score or they will miss the playoffs. Smith stumbles! Jones grabs the ball and races toward the Wolves' basket for a layup. Smith tackles him like a linebacker! Both of them slide across the floor and run into the wall behind the basket. It looks as if Jones might be injured! Players from both teams are shouting at each other. The referee has thrown Smith out of the game!

Does this scenario remind you of something you have seen during a high school, college, or professional basketball game? Or perhaps you have read about a similar incident. Actually, such an event took place in my experience. (The names have been changed to protect the guilty.) I was playing for my church team in a church league. I was the one who was tackled.

Does such an incident represent a Christian worldview of games? Surely most of us would answer with an emphatic, "No!" Unfortunately, though, too many Christians approach games with attitudes that appear to leave their Christian convictions out of the picture. Too many of us can tell stories involving Christians and games that don't align with a Christian worldview. I was often the one who allowed athletic intensity to overcome moral conviction in the midst of competition, and I have seen many of my friends do the same. Why? What is it about games that can encourage some of our most ungodly characteristics?

On the other hand, can sports bring out some of our most *godly* characteristics? Can God be glorified through games? At times in my life the exhilaration and concentration that can accompany games have included thankfulness to God. He gives me joy when I express my thankfulness to Him as I hit or throw a baseball, catch a football, shoot a basketball, volley a tennis ball, or hit a golf ball.

Arthur Holmes has written that "play is all-pervasive. It does not lie just on the fringes of life, as if games were spare parts we don't really need in the main business of the day."[1] If true, such a statement indicates the importance of our subject. It is worthy of our attention. Some people even believe that play is the defining characteristic of humans. "Nietzsche went so far as to reduce all of life and thought to masks in a play, taking nothing seriously except the will to power—in effect, the will to win—that all of life is a biologically driven power play."[2]

A Christian, of course, does not agree with this perspective, but the Christian does live in a world that tends to agree with Nietzsche's dictum. Many people definitely translate the "will to power" into "the will to win." Indeed, they often elaborate the phrase to mean "the will to win *at all costs.*" Vince Lombardi, the coach of the Green Bay Packers during their period of NFL domination, is famous for saying, "Winning isn't the main thing, it's the only thing." But, can the Christian play—win or lose—and not agree that winning is the only thing? If the answer is, "Yes!" the believer must realize that he has accepted a challenge to be Christ's ambassador even on the field of play.

A Brief History of Games

"That was an Olympian effort!"
"Those mountains have an Olympic grandeur."

Such expressions indicate some of the ways in which ancient games and their impact are part of our consciousness. Games were part of all ancient cultures. For some cultures, games were more sedentary than they were for other cultures, but a sense of play permeates man's history. The Greeks, who first held the Olympic Games and other similar events, organized those events approximately 3,500 years ago. All of them were dedicated to certain gods and were integrated with religious ceremonies. The competitors were originally amateurs whose only reward was a wreath or garland. Eventually, though, the rigorous training that was required led to their professional status. They received adulation in their cities and substantial prizes and monetary rewards.[3] As we will see, the New Testament contains metaphors relating to these games and competitors.

When the Romans became the dominant world power, they rejected the Greek emphasis on athletic skill because of the public nakedness of the competitors.[4] Such a response is ironic in light of the brutal games that soon came into vogue in the empire. Gladiatorial combat to the death, fights with beasts, even naval battles were staged in the arenas. The *Circus Maximus* in Rome, where important chariot races were held, probably held up to 250,000 people. "By A.D. 354 the games claimed 175 days out of the year."[5] Such popularity is indicative of a significant difference between the Greek and Roman attitudes about games. "The Greeks originally organized their games for the competitors, the Romans for the public. One was primarily competition, the other entertainment."[6]

The Roman thirst for barbaric spectacle and entertainment ultimately prompted the outrage of early church leaders. They "denounced the games and similar amusements because of idolatry, immodesty, and brutality. It was, in fact, the opposition of Christianity that brought them to an end."[7] Such a response may prove to be appropriate in our time. But, for the moment, I propose that we simply consider what Scripture contains to guide us in an appraisal of the games played by both Christians and non-Christians.

The Old Testament has few references to games, even though evidence of them can be found in all areas of the ancient Near East. "Simple and natural amusements and exercises, and trials of wit and wisdom, were more to the Hebrew taste."[8] The biblical text does mention children's games, sports such as running, archery, stone-lifting, high leaping, games of chance and skill, storytelling, dancing, the telling of proverbs, and riddles.[9] In addition, wrestling probably was part of Hebrew life.[10]

Of special interest is the joyous prophetic picture of Zechariah 8:5: "And the streets of the city will be filled with boys and girls playing in its streets." "The promise of the kingdom," as Lewis Smedes observes, "is of restored playfulness."[11] Evidently, play and games have a place in God's plan for His people:

> Scripture begins with life in a garden and ends with a city at play; so play—art and celebration and fun and games, and a

playful spirit—is part of our calling, part of the creation mandate. It is not the play of self-indulgence, nor of shed responsibility, but of gladness and celebration in responsible relationship to God."[11]

Games and the New Testament

Can you picture the apostle Paul as a sportswriter? Imagine him sitting in a stadium pressbox observing the athletes compete. Then imagine him writing his observations and opinions of what transpired. The next morning, you purchase a newspaper and turn to the sports section. There you find an account of the previous day's game under Paul's byline. Does this sound farfetched, out of character, and ludicrous? Actually, such a scenario is not far removed from Paul's knowledge of the games of his day. In several portions of his letters, one can find metaphors relating to athletic preparation and competition. The same is true for the writer of Hebrews. These New Testament writers evidently were aware of Greek and Roman games and realized that they could be used to teach valuable lessons to their readers. Their awareness is evidence that they were enmeshed in the surrounding culture, which was filled with indicators of the importance of games and competition in the ancient world.

These games "were so well known in Palestine and throughout the Roman Empire in the time of Christ and the apostles that they cannot be passed over in silence."[13] Archaeological remains indicate stadiums of various types in many cities, including Jerusalem, Jericho, Caesarea, Ephesus, Corinth, Rome, and Tarsus, the city of Paul's early life. "The early Christians, therefore, whether of Jewish or gentile origin, were able to understand, and the latter at any rate to appreciate, references either to the games in general, or to details of their celebration."[14] A brief survey of particular New Testament passages will provide us with a foundation for an analysis of games in contemporary life.

Some of the most intriguing athletic metaphors in all of Paul's writings are found in 1 Corinthians 9:24–27. He uses Greek terminology and images that stem directly from the athletic contests of his day, especially the triennial Isthmian Games held in Corinth. These terms and images include running a race to win, receiving a prize, competing, disciplining oneself in preparation for competition, concentrating, abiding by the rules, and even boxing. Variations on these themes can be found in Galatians 2:2 and 5:7; Philippians 2:16 and 3:14; and 2 Timothy 2:5 and 4:7. In Hebrews 12:1, the author of Hebrews echoes Paul's metaphors by encouraging Christians to "run with endurance the race that is set before us." In verse 2, he even refers to Jesus as the One who set the pace and has already covered the course.

These passages are worthy of many sermons and extensive commentary. Because that is not possible in this short chapter, let's consider a few insights from these biblical metaphors that are most germane to our subject.

1. There is no blanket condemnation of games. The metaphors carry the positive weight of someone who respected athletic endeavors.
2. There is much to learn about the Christian life when we compare it with games. Games can be seen and experienced in ways that correlate with Christian principles such as discipline, concentration, and perseverance.

3. These passages should not be gleaned uncritically. Surely Paul rejected many aspects of the games, such as the pagan religious emphases.

4. The physical body was not rejected as unimportant. Gnosticism, which was a prominent heresy of New Testament times, taught that the body was unimportant or even sinful. In contrast, these verses take the importance of the body for granted. It is God's creation.

Contemporary Views of Games

The Super Bowl. The Final Four. College bowl games. The Olympics. The NBA Finals. The World Series. Little League baseball. The Masters. The World Cup.

The list of such sports-related titles could fill several pages of this chapter because our culture is saturated with games. This infatuation takes a great deal of our time, attention, and money. An objective observer, in my opinion, would conclude that humans are obsessed with games. Current predictions and opinions of this infatuation vary from the skeptical to the optimistic.

Alvin Toffler, writing in 1970, predicted, "Leisure-time pursuits will become an increasingly important basis for differences between people, as the society shifts from a work orientation toward greater involvement in leisure. We shall advance into an era of breathtaking fun specialism."[15] Kareem Abdul-Jabbar, the great basketball player of the recent past, stated, "Modern sports is getting to be like professional wrestling; something is going awry."[16] According to Robert Higgs, author of *God in the Stadium,* "Professional sports is getting warped, and they carry a somber message to society in our contemporary times."[17] Higgs continued this theme by suggesting that "the idea of play and fun and enjoyment of the natural gifts of games is being warped by this incredible drive for money."[18] In comparing the games with a prize, such as the Super Bowl, Higgs concluded, "The more emphasis you put on the cultural prize, the bigger you make those prizes, the less regard and appreciation of the gift of the game itself, it seems to me."[19]

Do any of these opinions concur with your estimation of games? Are you one of the skeptics? If so, that probably is a sign that you have at least begun to ask if games are occupying the proper place in your life, your family's life, and the life of the culture at large. Before we become too cynical, though, let's consider more optimistic analyses.

In his book *The Culture of Narcissism,* Christopher Lasch draws a fascinating parallel between sports and our need for traditions and order. He believes that an intelligent sports spectator is one of the keys to a retention of the positive nature of games. He writes, "One of the virtues of contemporary sports lies in their resistance to the erosion of standards and their capacity to appeal to a knowledgeable audience."[20]

Michael Novak, who has written a thought-provoking book titled *The Joy of Sports,* juxtaposes European and American traditions around the place of sports in America's history. He believes that the "streets of America, unlike the streets of Europe, do not involve us in stories and anecdotes rich with a thousand years of human struggle. Sports are our chief civilizing agent. Sports are our most universal art form. Sports tutor us in the basic lived experiences of the humanist tradition."[21] Novak continues his praise with a statement that echoes the apostle Paul: "Play provides the fundamental metaphors and the paradigmatic experiences for understanding the other elements of life."[22]

Is there a happy medium between the skeptical and optimistic views of games? Or should we bring the two views together to find a wise perspective? Perhaps a coupling of the two views provides creative tension that enables us better to evaluate the place of games in the Christian life.

Christians in a Competitive World

> I believe that God made me for a purpose. For China. But He also made me fast. And when I run, I feel His pleasure. To give it up would be to hold Him in contempt. . . . To win is to honor Him.[23]

These poignant phrases are from *Chariots of Fire,* one of the truly great films. They were spoken by the actor who portrayed Eric Liddell, a great athlete and a great Christian. He is talking with his sister, who is pleading with him to fulfill his commitment to their mission in China. He was to fulfill that commitment, but first he considered it his duty to run in the 1924 Paris Olympics for the glory of God. When I first saw the film, I wept with joy and gratitude because of the film's portrayal of a man who understood and appreciated God's gift to him. In my estimation, the film—this scene in particular —contains a clear and eloquent statement of a Christian worldview as it applies to games, play, sports, or athletics. Keeping Eric Liddell's words in our minds, we can use the following principles to help us establish a foundation for a Christian's involvement in games.

1. "[P]lay is best seen as an attitude, a state of mind rather than as a distinguishable set of activities."[24]

One doesn't have to be involved in play to play; work can include an attitude of play as well.

2. "[P]lay is not the key to being human, but being human is the key to play."[25] And being human includes a free spirit that is "celebrative and imaginative because of the possibilities God has for us in this world."[26]

3. Play should instill "an attitude that carries over into all of life, finding joyful expression in whatever we do, productive or not."[27]

4. Play should be seen as an act of worship. "It is the religious meaning of life that gives purpose and meaning to both work and play. A responsible relationship to God includes play."[28]

You may be saying, "Okay, I can think on these things in solitude or in group discussion, but what about principles that will help me when I'm actually involved in games? How should I play?"

Application on the field is a challenge for many of us. Even Albert Camus, the existentialist writer, said that sports provided him with his "only lessons in ethics."[29] Thomas Aquinas "expressed three cautions that we would do well to observe nowadays. First, do not take pleasure in indecent or injurious play."[30] Think of a sold-out football stadium of people screaming their approval as an opponent lies immobile on the field. Such a reaction surely does not align with a Christian attitude toward games. "Second, do not lose your mental or emotional balance and self-control."[31] This may be one of the most challenging cautions. When we lose self-control during games, we are damaging what we say outside of games about our relationship with Christ. "Third, do not play in ways ill-fitting either the hour or the person."[32] When we play and how we honor God in the process speak loudly about the place of games in our lives.

So when we hear "Play ball!" or "Let the games begin!" or "Take your mark!" let us remember that whether we are participants or spectators, God can honor our games, but He requires a playful attitude that honors Him.

Endnotes

Chapter 1
1. Emil Brunner, *Christianity and Civilization* (London: Nisbet, 1948), 142.
2. H. Richard Niebuhr, *Christ and Culture* (New York: Harper & Row, 1951).
3. Donald G. Bloesch, *Freedom for Obedience* (San Francisco: Harper & Row, 1987), 227.
4. Charles E. Kinzie, "The Absorbed Church: Our Inheritance of Conformed Christianity," *Sojourners* 7 (July 1978): 22.
5. Ibid.
6. Harry Blamires, *The Christian Mind* (Ann Arbor, Mich.: Servant, 1963), 58.
7. Harry Blamires, *Recovering the Christian Mind* (Downers Grove, Ill.: InterVarsity, 1988), 59–60.
8. Carl F. H. Henry, *Christian Countermoves in a Decadent Culture* (Portland, Ore.: Multnomah, 1986), 32.
9. Charles H. Kraft, "Can Anthropological Insight Assist Evangelical Theology?" *The Christian Scholar's Review* 7 (1977): 182.
10. Bloesch, *Freedom for Obedience,* 244.
11. Julius Lipner, "Being One, Let Me Be Many: Facets of the Relationship Between the Gospel and Culture," *International Review of Missions* 74 (April 1985): 162.
12. Lesslie Newbigin, "Can the West Be Converted?" *Evangelical Review of Theology* 11 (October 1987): 366.
13. Emil Brunner, *Christianity and Civilization* (London: Nisbet & Co., 1948), 157.
14. Donald Bloesch, "The Legacy of Karl Barth," *TSF Bulletin* 9 (May–June 1986): 8.
15. Carl F. H. Henry, "The Crisis of Modern Learning," *Faculty Dialogue* 10 (winter 1988): 7.
16. Karl Barth, *Theology and Church,* trans. Louise Pettibone Smith (New York: Harper & Row, 1962), 349.
17. Joseph A. Hill, "Human Culture in Biblical Perspective," *Presbyterian Journal,* 18 February 1981, 9.
18. Stephen Mayor, "Jesus Christ and the Christian Understanding of Society," *Scottish Journal of Theology* 32 (1979): 59–60.

Chapter 2

1. The word *skill,* which is frequently employed to describe artisans in these chapters (NASB), is from the Hebrew word *hakam,* meaning "wise." One of its main synonyms is *bin,* basically meaning "discernment." Thus, the skillful person is one who, in the minds of the Israelites, was also "wise" and "discerning" in his artistry.
2. Gene Edward Veith, *The Gift of Art: The Place of the Arts in Scripture* (Downers Grove, Ill.: InterVarsity, 1983), 31.
3. Carl F. H. Henry, *Christian Personal Ethics* (Grand Rapids: Baker, 1957), 420.
4. Edward J. Young, *The Prophecy of Daniel* (Grand Rapids: Eerdmans, 1949), 48–49.
5. George Eldon Ladd, *A Theology of the New Testament* (Grand Rapids: Eerdmans, 1974). In particular, see chapters 17 and 29.
6. Ibid., 225.
7. Ibid.
8. Ibid.
9. Ibid., 226.
10. Ibid.
11. Everett F. Harrison, Geoffrey W. Bromiley, and Carl F. H. Henry, eds., *Baker's Dictionary of Theology* (Grand Rapids: Baker, 1960), s.v. "World, Worldliness," by Everett F. Harrison.
12. Ladd, *Theology of the New Testament,* 226.
13. Ibid., 227.
14. Ibid.
15. Ibid., 400.
16. R. C. Sproul, *The Holiness of God* (Wheaton, Ill.: Tyndale House, 1985), 209.
17. Ronald B. Allen, *The Majesty of Man: The Dignity of Being Human* (Portland, Ore.: Multnomah, 1984), 191.
18. Henry, *Christian Personal Ethics,* 420.
19. Ibid., 428.
20. F. W. Grosheide, *Commentary on the First Epistle to the Corinthians* (Grand Rapids: Eerdmans, 1953), 243.
21. Charles H. Kraft, *Christianity in Culture* (Maryknoll, N.Y.: Orbis, 1979), 103.
22. Ibid.

Chapter 3

1. James D. Hunter, *Culture Wars: The Struggle to Define America* (New York: Basic Books, 1991), 310.
2. *Dallas Morning News,* 30 October 1998, 7A.
3. William J. Bennett, *The De-Valuing of America* (Colorado Springs: Focus on the Family, 1994), 11.
4. Ibid.
5. Ibid.
6. Ibid., 12.
7. Ibid.

8. Francis A. Schaeffer, *How Should We Then Live?* (Old Tappan, N.J.: Revell, 1976), 205.

Chapter 4

1. James W. Sire, *The Universe Next Door,* 3d ed. (Downers Grove, Ill.: InterVarsity, 1997), 16.
2. W. Gary Phillips and William E. Brown, *Making Sense of Your World* (Chicago: Moody, 1991), 29.
3. Brian J. Walsh and J. Richard Middleton, *The Transforming Vision* (Downers Grove, Ill.: InterVarsity, 1984), 32.
4. Arthur F. Holmes, *Contours of a Worldview* (Grand Rapids: Eerdmans, 1983), 5.
5. Sire, *The Universe Next Door,* 17–18.
6. These are the chapter headings of Sire's book.

Chapter 5

1. All Scripture quoted in this chapter is taken from the *New American Standard Bible,* The Lockman Foundation, 1995.
2. Sharon Begley, John Carey, and Ray Sawhill, "How the Brain Works," *Newsweek,* 7 February 1983, 40.
3. See chapter 6 of this book for additional insights concerning E. O. Wilson.
4. Edward O. Wilson, "The Biological Basis of Morality," *The Atlantic Monthly,* April 1998, 54.
5. Quoted in Begley, Carey, and Sawhill, "How the Brain Works," 47.
6. *The Oxford Dictionary of Quotations* (London: OUP, 1962), 403 and referred to in Begley, Carey, and Sawhill, "How the Brain Works," 47.
7. Charles Habib Malik, "Your Mind Matters: Cultivate It," *Active Christians in Education,* January 1981, 1A.
8. R. Laird Harris, ed., *Theological Wordbook of the Old Testament,* vol. 1 (Chicago: Moody, 1980), 377.
9. J. P. Moreland, *Love Your God with All Your Mind* (Colorado Springs: Navpress, 1997), 39.
10. R. V. G. Tasker, *The Second Epistle of Paul to the Corinthians* (Grand Rapids: Eerdmans, 1963), 135.

Chapter 6

1. Stephen Moore, "The Growth of Government in America," *The Freeman,* April 1993, 124.
2. Marvin Olasky, *The Tragedy of American Compassion* (Washington, D.C.: Regnery, 1992), 174.
3. William Bennett, *The Index of Leading Cultural Indicators* (New York: Touchstone, 1994), 50.
4. *Terminator II: Judgment Day* (Carolco Pictures, Inc., 1991).
5. *Star Trek: The Motion Picture* (Paramount Pictures, 1980).

6. John Gerassi, *Jean-Paul Sartre: Hated Conscience of His Century* (Chicago: University of Chicago Press, 1989), 50.
7. Edward O. Wilson, *On Human Nature* (Cambridge, Mass.: Harvard University Press, 1978), 3.
8. Brugh W. Joy, *Joy's Way* (Los Angeles: J. B. Tarcher, 1979), 4.
9. Gerald G. Jampolsky, *Teach Only Love* (New York: Bantam, 1983), 52.
10. Bhagwan Shree Rajneesh, *I Am the Gate* (Philadelphia: Harper Colophon, 1977), 5.
11. Leslie Stevenson, *Seven Theories of Human Nature* (New York: Oxford University Press, 1987), 105.
12. *A Clockwork Orange* (Warner Bros., 1971).
13. Wilson, *On Human Nature,* 6.
14. Robert D. Cumming, *The Philosophy of Jean-Paul Sartre* (New York: Random House, 1965), 363.
15. Joy, *Joy's Way,* 7.
16. Rajneesh, *I Am the Gate,* 5.
17. Israel Shenker, "The Provocative Progress of a Pilgrim Polymath," *Smithsonian,* May 1993, 123.
18. Ibid.
19. *Flatliners* (Columbia Pictures, 1990).
20. Edward O. Wilson, *Naturalist* (Washington, D.C.: Island Press, 1994), 46.
21. William L. Craig, *Reasonable Faith: Christian Truth and Apologetics* (Wheaton, Ill.: Crossway, 1994), 71.
22. Ibid., 70.

Chapter 8

1. William D. Watkins, *The New Absolutes* (Minneapolis: Bethany House, 1996).
2. Ibid., 23.
3. Ibid., chap. 3.
4. Ibid., 65.
5. Ibid., 84–87.
6. Ibid., 49.
7. Ibid., 50ff.
8. Ibid., 55ff.
9. Ibid., 208–10.
10. Ibid., 207–8.
11. S. D. Gaede, *The New Absolutes: Political Correctness, Multi-Culturalism and the Future of Truth and Justice* (Downers Grove, Ill: InterVarsity, 1993), 21.
12. Ibid., 34.
13. Ibid., chap. 14.
14. Ibid., 240.

Chapter 9

1. C. Nolan Huizenga, "The Arts: A Bridge Between the Natural and Spiritual Realms," in *The Christian Imagination: Essays on Literature and the Arts,* ed. Leland Ryken (Grand Rapids: Baker, 1981), 70.

2. Nicholas Wolterstorff, *Art in Action* (Grand Rapids: Eerdmans, 1980), 4.
3. Ibid.
4. Frank E. Gaebelein, "Toward a Biblical View of Aesthetics," in *The Christian Imagination,* 48–49.

Chapter 10

1. John P. Newport, *Theology and Contemporary Art Forms* (Waco, Tex.: Word, 1971), 17–24.
2. Charles Garside Jr., *The Origins of Calvin's Theology of Music: 1536–1543* (Philadelphia: American Philosophical Society, 1979), 19.
3. *Zondervan Pictorial Dictionary,* s.v. "Music," by Harold M. Best and David Huttar.
4. Ibid.
5. Steve Lawhead, *Rock of This Age* (Downers Grove, Ill.: InterVarsity, 1987), 51–52.
6. Frank E. Gaebelein, "The Christian and Music," in *The Christian Imagination: Essays on Literature and the Arts,* ed. Leland Ryken (Grand Rapids: Baker, 1981), 446.
7. Harold M. Best, "Christian Responsibility in Music," in *The Christian Imagination,* 402.
8. Robert Elmore, "The Place of Music in Christian Life," in *The Christian Imagination,* 430.
9. Calvin M. Johansson, *Music and Ministry: A Biblical Counterpoint* (Peabody, Mass.: Hendrickson, 1984), 93–95.
10. Ibid., 412–13.
11. Erik Routley, *Church Music and the Christian Faith* (Carol Stream, Ill.: Agape, 1978), 89.
12. Kenneth Myers, *All God's Children and Blue Suede Shoes: Christians and Popular Culture* (Westchester, Ill.: Crossway, 1989), 59–64.
13. Steve Lawhead, *Turn Back the Night: A Christian Response to Popular Culture* (Westchester, Ill.: Crossway, 1978), 97.
14. Ibid., 98.

Chapter 11

1. "Letter to Higbald," as quoted in Eleanor S. Duckett, *Alcuin, Friend of Charlemagne* (New York: Macmillan, 1951), 209.
2. Tertullian, *On Against the Heretics,* chap. 7.
3. 2 Corinthians 6:14–15.
4. John Dixon Jr., *Nature and Grace in Art,* as quoted in Leland Ryken, *The Liberated Imagination* (Wheaton, Ill.: Shaw, 1989), 23.
5. Frank Kermode, ed. *The Selected Prose of T. S. Eliot* (NY: Harcourt Brace Jovanovich, 1975), 97–106.
6. Jeff Hanson, my coeditor, first articulated much of the material for this section in the March–April issue of *The Antithesis,* vol. 1, no. 2 (1995).

Chapter 12

1. Carl F. H. Henry, *Christian Personal Ethics* (Grand Rapids: Baker, 1957), 419.
2. Ibid.
3. Ibid., 428.

Chapter 13

1. Douglas Gomery, "As the Dial Turns," *Wilson Quarterly,* autumn 1993, 41.
2. Ibid.
3. Ibid.
4. Ibid.
5. Ibid., 41–42.
6. Ibid., 42.
7. John W. Kennedy, "Redeeming the Wasteland," *Christianity Today,* 2 October 1995, 92–102.
8. Quentin J. Schultze, *Redeeming Television* (Downers Grove, Ill.: InterVarsity, 1992), 28.
9. Malcolm Muggeridge, *Christ and the Media* (Grand Rapids: Eerdmans, 1977), 30.
10. Neil Postman, *Amusing Ourselves to Death* (New York: Viking Penguin, 1985), viii.
11. Kenneth A. Myers, *All God's Children and Blue Suede Shoes: Christians and Popular Culture* (Westchester, Ill.: Crossway, 1989), 157–77.
12. Clifford G. Christians, "Television: Medium Rare," *Pro Rege,* March 1990, 2.
13. Schultze, *Redeeming Television,* 28.
14. David Marc, "Understanding Television," *The Atlantic Monthly,* August 1984, 35–36.
15. Postman, *Amusing Ourselves to Death,* 9.
16. Ibid.
17. Christians, "Television: Medium Rare," 5.
18. Daniel J. Boorstin, *The Creators* (New York: Random House, 1992), 308–9.
19. Schultze, *Redeeming Television,* 94–95.

Chapter 14

1. "God and Television," *TV Guide,* March 29–April 4, 1997, 24–45.
2. "Angels and Insight," *TV Guide,* March 29–April 4, 1997, 43.
3. Ibid., 44.
4. Ibid., 55
5. Richard J. Neuhaus, *The Naked Public Square* (Grand Rapids: Eerdmans, 1984).
6. Larry Poland, *The Mediator* (Redlands, Calif.: Mastermedia International, 1997), 12: 1.

Chapter 15

1. Christopher Lasch, *The Culture of Narcissism: American Life in an Age of Diminishing Expectations* (New York: Warner, 1979), 23.
2. Charles R. Swindoll, *Living on the Ragged Edge* (Waco, Tex.: Word, 1985), 16.
3. Douglas D. Webster, *Selling Jesus: What's Wrong with Marketing the Church* (Downers Grove, Ill: InterVarsity, 1992), 68.
4. Rogier van Bakel, "This Space for Rent," *Wired,* June 1996, 160.
5. Webster, *Selling Jesus,* 29.

Chapter 16

1. Arthur Holmes, *Contours of a World View* (Grand Rapids: Eerdmans, 1983), 226.
2. Ibid.
3. *Encyclopaedia Britannica,* 15th ed., s.v. "Athletic Games and Contests."
4. Ibid.
5. *Wycliffe Bible Encyclopaedia,* s.v. "Games."
6. *Encyclopaedia Britannica.*
7. *Wycliffe Bible Encyclopaedia.*
8. *The International Standard Bible Encyclopaedia,* s.v. "Games."
9. Ibid.
10. *The New Bible Dictionary,* s.v. "Games."
11. Lewis Smedes, quoted in Holmes, *Contours of a World View,* 230.
12. Ibid., 231.
13. *The International Standard Bible Encyclopaedia.*
14. Ibid.
15. Alvin Toffler, *Future Shock* (New York: Bantam, 1970), 289.
16. Kareem Abdul-Jabbar, quoted by Robert Higgs, on Mars Hill Tapes, May–June 1996, vol. 21, ed. Ken Myers (Charlottesville, Va.: Mars Hill Tapes, 1996).
17. Ibid.
18. Ibid.
19. Ibid.
20. Christopher Lasch, *The Culture of Narcissism* (New York: Warner, 1979), 190.
21. Michael Novak, *The Joy of Sports* (New York: Basic Books, 1976), 27.
22. Ibid., 34.
23. David Puttnam, producer, *Chariots of Fire* (Burbank, Calif.: Warner Home Video, 1991).
24. Holmes, *Contours of a World View,* 224.
25. Ibid., 228.
26. Ibid., 231.
27. Ibid.
28. Ibid., 228.
29. Albert Camus, quoted in Novale, *The Joy of Sports,* 172.
30. Thomas Aquinas, quoted in Holmes, *Contours of a World View,* 231.
31. Ibid.
32. Ibid.

Other great books
in this series include . . .

Marriage, Family, and Sexuality
Kerby Anderson general editor
ISBN 0-8254-2031-8

Creation, Evolution, and Modern Science
Ray Bohlin, general editor
ISBN 0-8254-2033-4

Kids, Classrooms, and Contemporary Education
Don Closson, general editor
ISBN 0-8254-2034-2

Available at your local Christian bookstore or at

kregel
PUBLICATIONS

PO Box 2607, Grand Rapids, Michigan 49501